C000020855

Family Resources Survey

Great Britain 1999-2000

Editorial Team

Steve Ellerd-Elliott

Elaine Horsfall

Neil Butt

Naina Dhanecha

Ed Pickering

Corporate Document Services

Application for reproduction should be made in writing to The Copyright Unit, Her Majesty's Stationery Office, St Clements House, 2–16 Colegate, Norwich NR3 1BQ.

First published 2001

ISBN 1 84123 367 6

Printed by Biddles Limited.

Chapters 1, 8

Contents

DSS, Family Resources Survey Great Britain 1999-2000, © Crown Copyright 2001

DSS, Family Resources Survey Great Britain 1999-2000, © Crown Copyright 2001

Chapter 1

Introduction

Background

This is the seventh report providing information collected from the Family Resources Survey (FRS) and covers the period from April 1999 to the end of March 2000.

The FRS was launched in October 1992 to meet the information requirements of Department of Social Security (DSS) analysts. Traditionally, the Department had relied on other government social surveys, notably the Family Expenditure Survey (FES) and General Household Survey. However, these surveys have relatively small sample sizes and therefore did not provide sufficiently reliable information on many groups in society which were of particular interest to the DSS.

Households interviewed in the survey are asked a wide range of questions about their circumstances. Although some of the information collected is available elsewhere, the FRS provides new or much more detailed information in a number of areas and brings some topics together on one survey for the first time. The sample size allows more confidence in the analyses of smaller sub groups, including, for example, regional breakdowns and recipients of certain benefits.

Although the FRS was designed with the DSS's needs specifically in mind, it also contains information that is of interest to other government departments and outside researchers. This report provides a summary of findings for 1999-2000. The database from which it is derived has been deposited at the Data Archive at Essex University and is being made available directly to other government departments such as the Department of the Environment, Transport and the Regions and the Office for National Statistics.

Data collected

Modeling Social Security benefit entitlement is central to many of the DSS uses of FRS information and the data collected reflects this; focusing on income, including receipt of Social Security benefits, housing costs and circumstances of household members such as whether someone gives or receives care or has child care costs.

This focus also underlies the routeing of some questions. For example, detailed questions on the value of liquid assets held are only asked of those respondents who are willing to provide an estimate of the value of their total savings and report a figure between £1,500 and £20,000. Around a third of households surveyed fall into this category. This range is wide enough to capture those who may be entitled to benefit on the basis of their capital but reduces the burden on the majority of respondents.

Further questions address other areas relevant to DSS policy such as barriers to moving off benefits and into work, pension provision and maintenance payment and receipt.

The final section of this report summarises the information collected on the survey.

Contents of the report

The 1999-2000 report is similar in presentation to that for previous years. The aim continues to be to present the information in a clear and systematic way, as far as possible being consistent with other DSS publications. It retains the streamlined approach of the 1998-1999 report, with explanatory notes to the tables given at the start of each chapter. These notes also describe any changes to the tables. Analyses which set the results of the survey in context are available in other publications such as the Department's Households Below Average Income report and compendia publications produced by the Office for National Statistics such as Social and Regional Trends and the Social Focus series.

The structure of the report is as follows:

- Chapter 2 provides an overview of households, benefit units and individuals.

- Chapter 3 looks at income and benefits. Tables are shown on both a household and benefit unit basis and aim to exploit the detailed information which is collected by the FRS in this area.

- Chapter 4 considers tenure and housing costs. Although primarily a survey of incomes, the FRS collects detailed information on this aspect of expenditure.

- Chapter 5 looks at assets and savings. Like other surveys, the FRS collects information on the interest received on various types of investments. However, unlike most, for some respondents it also attempts to collect information on the actual value of holdings.

- Chapter 6 looks at carers and those needing care.

- Chapter 7 looks at employment, including non-financial benefits paid to employees and costs of being in work.

- Chapter 8 gives information on the sample, data collection and processing.

Main Changes for 1999-2000

The most important change in this year's survey is the rotation of questions. Certain questions are now asked every other year, rather than every year. This has been introduced in order to reduce the length of the questionnaire and the burden on respondents. For 1999-2000, questions on NHS treatment and travel to work costs have been rotated off. For 2000-01, these questions will be reinstated and questions on vehicle ownership and consumer durables rotated off.

DSS analysts concluded that they did not need the finer detail of children's savings, both in the Benefit Unit questionnaire and the Assets block. These questions have therefore been removed. This means that Chapter 5: Assets and Savings now only covers accounts held by Adults.

Government departments using the FRS 'care' data showed concern that the FRS seems to record fewer people giving or receiving care than the General Household Survey. Interviewer feedback also highlighted that some of the questions are difficult for interviewers and/or respondents. To address these concerns the care questions have been changed and this has affected the contents of Chapter 6: Carers.

Since October 1999, Family Credit – the benefit for working parents on low income - has been phased out, and replaced with the new Working Families' Tax Credit, administered

by, the Inland Revenue rather than the DSS. The same is true for Disability Working Allowance which has been replaced by Disabled Persons' Tax Credit. From October 2000 they can be received through the wage packet, as a tax adjustment, rather than as a cash benefit. However, for the first year the Inland Revenue continued to pay people the benefit as before, by cheque or direct credit. These are both combined with the previous benefit within our tables.

There has also been a definitional change to bring a person's employment status in line with the classical ILO definition. Individuals between the state pension age and the age of 70 who are looking for work are now asked whether or not they are able to start in the next two weeks. Previously they were classified as 'inactive' by default.

For more details on changes please see the introduction to each chapter.

Units and presentation

Throughout the report, tables refer to either households, benefit units or individuals. The definition of a household used in the FRS is "a single person or group of people living at the same address who either share one meal a day or share the living accommodation, ie a living room". So, for example, a group of students with a shared living room would be counted as a single household even if they did not eat together, but a group of bedsits at the same address would not.

A household will consist of one or more benefit units, which in turn consists of a number of individuals (adults and children). "Benefit unit" is a standard DSS term which relates to the tighter family definition of "a single adult or couple living as married and any dependent children". A dependent child is aged under 16 or under 19 if still in full time non-advanced education. So, for example, a man and wife living with their young children and an elderly parent would be one household but two benefit units. It should be noted that "benefit unit" is used throughout the publication as a description of groups of individuals regardless of whether they are in receipt of any Social Security benefits.

Figures for percentages based on sample estimates have been reweighted so that they apply to the overall population. This involves the use of a set of adjustment factors which attempt to correct for differential non-response at the same time as they scale up sample estimates. These factors take into account demographic variables such as age, sex and marital status together with region and tenure. Tables give unweighted sample counts for *base=100%* figures to help users to judge the robustness of the information (the larger the sample size, the more robust the relevant percentage figure).

Information on variables and data items tabulated in the report is provided in the Glossary. It should be stressed that definitions of items such as gross income and its components might differ from those used in other publications and from those used in FRS reports for 1997-98 and earlier. More details are given in Chapter 8.

Uses of Family Resources Survey Data

Although primary users of FRS data remain within the DSS, the survey is increasingly being used outside the Department.

FRS data are incorporated in to the Policy Simulation Model (PSM), used extensively by DSS economists for policy evaluation and costing of policy options. Responses are uprated to current prices, benefits and earnings levels and calibrated to DSS Departmental Report forecasts of benefit caseload and expenditure. Using FRS data has made it possible to model some aspects of the benefit system which could not be done previously,: eg income related benefits' severe disability premiums and allowances for child care costs.

In addition to incorporation in formal modelling, FRS data play a vital role in the analysis of patterns of benefit receipt for policy monitoring and evaluation and benefit forecasting. Examples are the extent of multiple benefit receipt and the distribution of individual benefits.

Data are also used in figures for take-up of income related benefits. Figures are based on a combination of administrative and survey data. The aim of the analysis of FRS data is to establish how many interviewees who say they are not receiving benefits actually appear to be entitled to them. The access to metadata, especially on imputation, also informs analysts' judgements.

FRS data are analysed in order to produce analyses of incomes using Households Below Average Income (HBAI) methodology. The income measure used is based on weekly net (disposable) equivalised household income (ie income adjusted for household size and composition by means of equivalence scales). The HBAI data set also forms the basis of the Pensioners' Income Series, the Department's analysis of trends in components and levels of pensioners' incomes.

The FRS has also been used as a sampling frame for follow up studies to look at particular groups. The most recent example is the elderly follow-up survey of entitled non-recipients, which took place between mid-March 1998 and end-April 1998. The survey remit was to try and establish why these individuals were not claiming benefits to which they were entitled. The largest example is the Disability Survey, which re-interviewed over 7,000 disabled respondents who appeared in the FRS between July 1996 and March 1997. The survey provides a detailed picture of type and severity of disability, extra needs and participation in leisure activities of the disabled. Merged with FRS information, a major use of the results by DSS is to measure and analyse receipt of disability benefits and gather information to enable more accurate forecasting of expenditure.

The data set is provided to other government departments on request. It is also accessed by researchers and analysts outside government through the Data Archive at Essex University.

Rounding and accuracy

The tables in this report show the results after validation and imputation for item non-response, and after adjustment for unit non-response using weights which control for a number of factors. However, validation can only be effective where it is possible to correct the response, for example by referring to interviewers' notes. Weighting can only correct for known non-response biases and results are sensitive to the values of control variables used to generate the weights.

Therefore, although work has been undertaken to try and ensure that the figures which have been collected are valid and that adjustments are made for non-response, problems will remain. For example, comparisons of benefit recipients on the survey with administrative data still show a mismatch following weighting. This may be partly due to misreporting of certain data items and sampling error but also may reflect non-response biases not controlled for in the weighting factors. Efforts are continually being made to minimise these problems, for example through greater reliance on documentary evidence at the interview and maintaining response rates. More information on FRS non-response and data quality is given in Chapter 8.

In the tables which follow, the following conventions have been used:

0   nil

-   negligible

.   not available because of small sample sizes

Individual figures have been rounded independently. Therefore the sum of component items do not necessarily add to the totals shown.

Acknowledgements

Thanks go once again to all the respondents in households across Great Britain who agreed to be interviewed; to the interviewers at the Office for National Statistics and the National Centre for Social Research and colleagues in those organisations; to those who have contributed towards this publication both through providing figures and checking of the content; and to our computing support team here in ASD.

Contact points

If you would like further information on the FRS please contact:

ASD3E
Department of Social Security
The Adelphi
1-11 John Adam Street
London
WC2N 6HT

Telephone: 020 7962 8991

Any comments on the presentation and content of this and future reports should also be sent to this address.

You can also find background to the FRS on the internet.

Please go to ***www.dss.gov.uk*** or look at the National Statistics website on ***www.statistics.gov.uk***

Household characteristics

Introduction

Chapter 2 contains information on the main characteristics of households, benefit units and individuals. These characteristics are used as the units of measurements throughout the remainder of the report.

Information is given on a household, benefit unit and individual basis with splits for age, ethnic group, sex and region.

The information shown is important for interpreting tables in other chapters of the report. Characteristics such as size and age distribution of the household will have an effect on, for example, income and housing costs. Chapter 8 contains further information on the nature of the sample and data quality.

Contents and points to note when interpreting tables

Tables 2.1 to 2.7 analyse households by size, region, age of head and ethnic group of head. Tables showing the composition of households are extended to include, for example, households with one or more sick or disabled adults under pension age.

Tables 2.8 to 2.10 show households by access to consumer durables and by Council Tax band. Different Council Tax bands exist for England, Wales and Scotland and more details of the differences are given in the Glossary. Note that the questions about consumer durables on the FRS ask about access rather than ownership. For example, a household may have access to a washing machine but not own it. With the exception of telephones, items available for communal use are included only if they can be used in the respondent's accommodation. These data are also split by region and household composition.

Tables 2.11 to 2.19 look at benefit units by family and economic status, region, age, ethnic group and marital status of head.

Table 2.20 provides analysis of individuals by sex, age, and region.

Key definitions used
(for a full explanation of all definitions please refer to the Glossary)

- Council Tax band
- Economic status
- Ethnic group
- Family status

- Head of household
- Head of benefit unit
- Marital status
- Sick or disabled adults

Changes to tables between 1998-1999 and 1999-2000

The questions on types of NHS treatment and services have been rotated off the survey in 1999-2000 (see Introduction).

This means that Table 2.21 (Individuals by medical treatment, age and sex) does not appear in this report, but will return next year.

Table 2.1: Households by size and region

			Government Office Region			
Size	North East	North West and Merseyside	Yorkshire and the Humber	East Midlands	West Midlands	Eastern
1 person	31	28	29	26	28	26
2 persons	33	35	35	38	35	39
3 persons	17	16	15	16	16	16
4 persons	12	14	14	14	14	13
5 persons	5	5	5	4	5	4
6 persons	1	1	1	1	1	1
7 or more persons	-	1	1	-	1	-
Average number of persons per household	**2.30**	**2.40**	**2.39**	**2.37**	**2.41**	**2.36**
Total households (base=100%)	**1,284**	**3,064**	**2,242**	**1,796**	**2,234**	**2,411**

Table 2.1: Continued

			Government Office Region			**Great**
Size	London	South East	South West	England	Wales	Scotland	**Britain**
1 person	33	26	30	28	27	33	**29**
2 persons	30	38	39	36	36	34	**36**
3 persons	15	15	13	15	17	16	**16**
4 persons	14	14	12	13	13	13	**13**
5 persons	5	5	4	5	5	4	**5**
6 persons	2	1	1	1	2	1	**1**
7 or more persons	1	-	-	1	-	-	**1**
Average number of persons per household	**2.38**	**2.39**	**2.28**	**2.37**	**2.40**	**2.26**	**2.37**
Total households (base=100%)	**2,661**	**3,529**	**2,226**	**21,447**	**1,358**	**2,183**	**24,988**

Table 2.2: Households by ethnic group of head and size

| | | | Number of persons | | | | | |
Ethnic group	One	Two	Three	Four	Five	Six	Seven or more	Total households (base=100%)
White	29	36	16	13	4	1	-	23,760
Black	35	28	15	14	6	1	1	438
Indian	11	22	19	24	15	5	4	236
Pakistani/Bangladeshi	10	11	15	17	17	11	19	248
Other	24	30	15	19	7	3	2	306
Total households	**29**	**36**	**16**	**13**	**5**	**1**	**1**	**24,988**

Table 2.3: Households by age of head and size

Percentage of households

| | | | Number of persons | | | | | |
Age	One	Two	Three	Four	Five	Six	Seven or more	Total households (base=100%)
16 to 19	45	37	11	4	3	0	0	111
20 to 24	26	40	21	10	2	1	-	748
25 to 29	27	38	20	11	4	1	-	1,715
30 to 34	24	26	19	20	7	2	1	2,402
35 to 39	18	19	18	29	11	4	1	2,655
40 to 44	16	18	19	29	13	3	2	2,330
45 to 49	18	23	23	25	9	2	1	2,099
50 to 54	19	37	23	16	4	1	-	2,355
55 to 59	21	49	21	7	2	1	-	1,866
60 to 64	24	59	12	4	1	-	-	1,880
65 to 69	37	53	8	2	1	-	-	1,923
70 to 74	46	48	4	1	-	-	-	1,750
75 to 79	55	41	3	1	-	-	-	1,609
80 to 84	66	31	3	1	0	-	0	883
85 or over	75	23	1	0	-	-	0	662
Total households	**29**	**36**	**16**	**13**	**5**	**1**	**1**	**24,988**

Table 2.4: Households by age of head and region

		Government Office Region				
Age	North East	North West and Merseyside	Yorkshire and the Humber	East Midlands	West Midlands	Eastern
16 to 19	1	-	1	-	-	-
20 to 24	4	3	4	3	3	4
25 to 29	6	7	7	7	7	7
30 to 34	9	9	10	10	10	9
35 to 39	10	10	10	9	9	9
40 to 44	10	10	9	9	8	9
45 to 49	7	10	8	9	9	7
50 to 54	11	9	10	11	10	11
55 to 59	8	8	8	8	8	9
60 to 64	8	8	8	7	8	7
65 to 69	8	8	7	7	7	8
70 to 74	6	7	7	7	7	7
75 to 79	5	6	6	6	7	6
80 to 84	4	3	3	3	4	3
85 or over	2	2	2	2	2	3
Total households (base=100%)	1,284	3,064	2,242	1,796	2,234	2,411

Table 2.4: Continued

		Government Office Region					**Great**
Age	London	South East	South West	England	Wales	Scotland	**Britain**
16 to 19	-	1	-	-	1	1	1
20 to 24	3	3	3	3	4	4	3
25 to 29	10	7	6	7	7	8	7
30 to 34	13	9	9	10	8	9	10
35 to 39	12	10	9	10	7	11	10
40 to 44	9	9	8	9	8	10	9
45 to 49	8	10	8	9	9	8	9
50 to 54	9	11	10	10	10	9	10
55 to 59	8	8	8	8	8	9	8
60 to 64	5	8	7	7	9	8	7
65 to 69	6	8	8	7	8	7	7
70 to 74	5	6	8	7	8	7	7
75 to 79	5	6	7	6	7	6	6
80 to 84	3	3	4	3	4	3	3
85 or over	2	3	4	3	2	2	2
Total households (base=100%)	2,661	3,529	2,226	21,447	1,358	2,183	24,988

Table 2.5: Households by composition and region

Percentage of households

Household composition	North East	North West and Merseyside	Yorkshire and the Humber	East Midlands	West Midlands	Eastern
Households without children						
One adult						
adult male over pension age	4	4	4	3	4	3
adult female over pension age	12	11	12	10	12	11
adult male under pension age	11	9	9	9	9	8
adult female under pension age	5	4	5	5	4	4
Two adults						
both over pension age	9	9	8	10	9	12
one over pension age	6	5	5	5	5	5
both under pension age	16	17	19	20	18	20
Three or more adults	9	9	8	10	11	10
Households with children						
One adult						
one child	3	3	2	2	3	2
two children	2	2	2	1	2	2
three or more children	2	1	2	1	1	1
Two adults						
one child	7	7	6	8	6	6
two children	7	8	9	9	9	9
three or more children	3	4	5	4	4	4
Three or more adults						
one child	2	3	2	2	2	2
two children	2	1	1	1	1	1
three or more children	-	1	1	-	-	-
Total households without children	72	69	70	72	71	73
Total households with children	28	31	30	28	29	27
Households with one or more adults over pension age	32	32	31	31	33	33
Households with one or more sick or disabled adults under pension age	28	25	23	22	22	19
Households with one or more unemployed adults under pension age	7	6	7	5	6	5

DSS, Family Resources Survey Great Britain 1999-2000, © Crown Copyright 2001

Table 2.5: Continued

Government Office Region

Household composition	London	South East	South West	England	Wales	Scotland	Great Britain
Households without children							
One adult							
adult male over pension age	4	3	3	3	3	3	**3**
adult female over pension age	9	10	13	11	11	12	**11**
adult male under pension age	13	9	9	10	9	11	**10**
adult female under pension age	7	4	4	5	3	7	**5**
Two adults							
both over pension age	7	10	12	9	11	8	**9**
one over pension age	4	5	5	5	6	5	**5**
both under pension age	17	21	20	19	16	18	**19**
Three or more adults	9	9	7	9	11	9	**9**
Households with children							
One adult							
one child	3	2	2	3	3	3	**3**
two children	3	1	2	2	2	2	**2**
three or more children	2	1	1	1	1	1	**1**
Two adults							
one child	7	7	6	7	7	6	**7**
two children	8	9	8	9	8	7	**8**
three or more children	3	4	4	4	4	3	**4**
Three or more adults							
one child	3	2	2	3	3	3	**3**
two children	2	1	1	1	1	1	**1**
three or more children	1	-	-	1	-	-	**1**
Total households without children	**69**	**71**	**73**	**71**	**71**	**73**	**71**
Total households with children	**31**	**29**	**27**	**29**	**29**	**27**	**29**
Households with one or more adults over pension age	*27*	*31*	*35*	*31*	*36*	*30*	*31*
Households with one or more sick or disabled adults under pension age	*21*	*18*	*20*	*22*	*27*	*24*	*22*
Households with one or more unemployed adults under pension age	*7*	*4*	*4*	*6*	*6*	*8*	*6*

Table 2.6: Households by composition and ethnic group of head

Percentage of households

| Household composition | Ethnic group | | | | | Total households |
	White	Black	Indian	Pakistani/ Bangladeshi	Other	
Households without children						
One adult						
adult male over pension age	3	4	2	1	1	3
adult female over pension age	11	4	2	1	3	11
adult male under pension age	9	19	7	6	13	10
adult female under pension age	5	8	1	2	7	5
Two adults						
both over pension age	10	3	2	1	3	9
one over pension age	5	3	1	1	3	5
both under pension age	19	13	18	7	18	19
Three or more adults	9	6	15	10	9	9
Households with children						
One adult						
one child	2	9	1	1	5	3
two children	2	6	2	4	3	2
three or more children	1	4	1	3	1	1
Two adults						
one child	7	5	9	7	6	7
two children	8	8	13	10	12	8
three or more children	3	5	9	21	6	4
Three or more adults						
one child	3	2	11	5	4	3
two children	1	1	5	7	2	1
three or more children	-	1	3	13	2	1
Total households without children	72	60	47	29	57	71
Total households with children	28	40	53	71	43	29
Households with one or more adults over pension age	32	17	16	15	14	31
Households with one or more sick or disabled adults under pension age	22	22	31	43	22	22
Households with one or more unemployed adults under pension age	6	14	12	18	8	6

Table 2.7: Households by ethnic group of head and region

			Government Office Region			
Ethnic group	North East	North West and Merseyside	Yorkshire and the Humber	East Midlands	West Midlands	Eastern
White	99	96	96	95	94	98
Black	0	1	1	1	2	-
Indian	-	1	-	3	2	-
Pakistani/Bangladeshi	-	2	2	-	1	-
Other	-	1	1	1	1	1
Total households (base=100%)	1,284	3,064	2,242	1,796	2,234	2,411

Table 2.7: Continued

Percentage of households

			Government Office Region			Great
Ethnic group	London	South East	South West	England	Wales	Scotland	**Britain**
White	78	97	99	94	98	99	**95**
Black	10	1	-	2	-	-	**2**
Indian	3	1	-	1	-	0	1
Pakistani/Bangladeshi	4	-	-	1	-	-	1
Other	6	1	-	1	1	1	1
Total households (base=100%)	2,661	3,529	2,226	21,447	1,358	2,183	24,988

Table 2.8: Households by access to consumer durables and region

Consumer durables	North East	North West and Merseyside	Yorkshire and the Humber	East Midlands	West Midlands	Eastern
Satellite dish/cable	33	33	28	31	30	31
Video recorder	85	86	85	87	86	87
Deep Freeze or Fridge/freezer	92	93	92	94	93	94
Washing machine	92	91	93	94	92	93
Tumble dryer	46	51	51	55	53	55
Dishwasher	14	20	18	23	20	30
Microwave	85	82	83	84	82	81
Telephone	93	95	95	96	96	97
Compact disc player	67	71	69	72	69	75
Home computer	29	35	32	36	35	40
Cars/light vans	61	69	66	74	72	79
Central heating	95	84	83	92	86	92
Television	99	98	99	99	98	98
Total households (base=100%)	1,284	3,064	2,242	1,796	2,234	2,411

Table 2.8: Continued

Consumer durables	London	South East	South West	England	Wales	Scotland	**Great Britain**
Satellite dish/cable	32	30	26	30	33	30	**30**
Video recorder	82	88	83	85	84	86	**85**
Deep Freeze or Fridge/freezer	91	94	93	93	94	90	**93**
Washing machine	86	92	90	91	92	94	**91**
Tumble dryer	42	56	51	51	48	52	**51**
Dishwasher	25	34	26	24	20	21	**24**
Microwave	71	81	78	80	84	82	**80**
Telephone	96	97	97	96	94	94	**96**
Compact disc player	69	77	70	71	65	74	**71**
Home computer	41	46	36	38	32	31	**37**
Cars/light vans	61	79	76	71	71	62	**70**
Central heating	91	92	86	89	91	92	**89**
Television	97	98	99	98	99	98	**98**
Total households (base=100%)	2,661	3,529	2,226	21,447	1,358	2,183	24,988

DSS, Family Resources Survey Great Britain 1999-2000, © Crown Copyright 2001

Table 2.9: Households by composition and access to consumer durables

Percentage of households

Consumer durables

Household composition	Satellite dish/cable	Video recorder	Deep Freeze or Fridge/freezer	Washing machine	Tumble dryer	Dishwasher	Microwave	Telephone
Households without children								
One adult								
adult male over pension age	14	53	78	66	27	7	57	89
adult female over pension age	6	53	85	78	27	7	63	97
adult male under pension age	26	78	81	76	32	9	68	85
adult female under pension age	16	79	84	86	37	12	76	94
Two adults								
both over pension age	18	83	95	94	46	20	75	99
one over pension age	26	91	95	96	52	24	82	98
both under pension age	35	94	96	97	57	29	88	98
Three or more adults	43	95	98	98	61	32	89	98
Households with children								
One adult								
one child	28	90	94	94	45	10	82	89
two children	35	90	94	97	53	14	80	90
three or more children	36	88	96	94	57	14	81	83
Two adults								
one child	43	97	98	99	66	34	91	98
two children	45	98	99	99	70	42	91	98
three or more children	50	97	99	99	73	42	90	97
Three or more adults								
one child	55	97	99	99	68	39	94	99
two children	48	98	99	99	72	44	91	98
three or more children	41	93	99	98	58	29	85	97
Total households without children	**25**	**81**	**91**	**89**	**45**	**20**	**77**	**96**
Total households with children	**43**	**96**	**98**	**98**	**65**	**34**	**89**	**96**
Households with one or more adults over pension age	*16*	*72*	*90*	*86*	*39*	*16*	*71*	*97*
Households with one or more sick or disabled adults under pension age	*36*	*88*	*93*	*92*	*53*	*21*	*84*	*93*
Households with one or more unemployed adults under pension age	*30*	*84*	*91*	*88*	*46*	*16*	*77*	*87*

Table 2.9: Continued

Household composition	Consumer durables					Total households (base=100%)
	Compact disc player	Home computer	Cars/light vans	Central heating	Television	
Households without children						
One adult						
adult male over pension age	28	8	46	80	96	1,019
adult female over pension age	21	3	21	86	99	2,869
adult male under pension age	72	32	60	84	95	1,963
adult female under pension age	71	24	56	85	96	1,400
Two adults						
both over pension age	48	14	74	90	99	2,561
one over pension age	64	24	78	88	99	1,178
both under pension age	86	46	87	91	99	4,340
Three or more adults	89	53	87	91	99	1,656
Households with children						
One adult						
one child	80	28	42	87	99	807
two children	79	34	46	87	99	663
three or more children	74	26	33	86	99	364
Two adults						
one child	92	58	88	92	99	1,880
two children	93	66	92	95	99	2,375
three or more children	86	60	87	91	98	1,070
Three or more adults						
one child	93	66	91	94	100	512
two children	91	67	88	94	100	224
three or more children	75	47	77	87	99	107
Total households without children	**64**	**29**	**67**	**88**	**98**	16,986
Total households with children	**89**	**56**	**80**	**92**	**99**	8,002
Households with one or more adults over pension age	*41*	*13*	*54*	*87*	*99*	*8,225*
Households with one or more sick or disabled adults under pension age	*75*	*37*	*68*	*88*	*98*	*5,228*
Households with one or more unemployed adults under pension age	*75*	*36*	*57*	*85*	*98*	*1,309*

Table 2.10: Households by Council Tax band and region

			Government Office Region			
Council Tax band	North East	North West and Merseyside	Yorkshire and the Humber	East Midlands	West Midlands	Eastern
Band A	61	43	46	37	34	15
Band B	15	19	19	23	23	22
Band C	11	16	16	18	18	22
Band D	7	10	8	12	11	20
Band E	3	6	5	5	7	10
Band F	1	3	3	3	4	5
Band G	1	2	1	1	2	4
Band H	-	-	-	-	-	1
Not valued separately	1	1	1	1	1	1
Total households						
(base=100%)	**1,284**	**3,064**	**2,242**	**1,796**	**2,234**	**2,411**

Table 2.10: Continued

			Government Office Region			Great
Council Tax band	London	South East	South West	England	Wales	Scotland	**Britain**
Band A	3	9	17	26	20	25	**26**
Band B	14	15	23	19	26	27	**20**
Band C	25	23	23	20	20	14	**19**
Band D	27	23	17	16	15	11	**16**
Band E	14	14	9	9	9	11	**9**
Band F	7	8	5	5	5	6	**5**
Band G	7	6	3	3	2	4	**3**
Band H	1	1	-	1	-	-	**1**
Not valued separately	2	2	2	1	2	1	**1**
Total households							
(base=100%)	**2,661**	**3,529**	**2,226**	**21,447**	**1,358**	**2,183**	**24,988**

Table 2.11: Number of benefit units per household by region

			Government Office Region			
Number of benefit units	North East	North West and Merseyside	Yorkshire and the Humber	East Midlands	West Midlands	Eastern
1 benefit unit	80	80	84	83	80	82
2 benefit units	15	15	12	13	15	14
3 benefit units	4	4	3	4	5	3
4 benefit units	1	1	1	-	-	1
5 benefit units	0	-	-	-	-	-
6 benefit units	0	-	0	0	-	-
7 benefit units	0	0	-	0	-	0
Average number of benefit units per household	1.25	1.26	1.22	1.22	1.26	1.22
Total households (base=100%)	1,284	3,064	2,242	1,796	2,234	2,411

Table 2.11: Continued

			Government Office Region			**Great**
Number of benefit units	London	South East	South West	England	Wales	Scotland	**Britain**
1 benefit unit	77	82	86	81	78	80	**81**
2 benefit units	17	14	11	14	17	15	**14**
3 benefit units	5	3	3	4	4	4	**4**
4 benefit units	1	-	-	1	1	1	**1**
5 benefit units	-	-	-	-	-	0	**-**
6 benefit units	0	-	-	-	0	0	**-**
7 benefit units	0	0	0	-	0	0	**-**
Average number of benefit units per household	1.31	1.23	1.18	1.24	1.27	1.25	**1.25**
Total households (base=100%)	2,661	3,529	2,226	21,447	1,358	2,183	**24,988**

DSS, Family Resources Survey Great Britain 1999-2000, © Crown Copyright 2001

Table 2.12: Benefit units by family status and region

Family status	North East	North West and Merseyside	Yorkshire and the Humber	East Midlands	West Midlands	Eastern
			Government Office Region			
Pensioner couple	8	9	8	10	9	11
Single male pensioner	4	3	3	3	4	3
Single female pensioner	12	11	11	10	11	10
Couple with children	16	18	19	19	17	18
Couple without children	20	19	22	24	21	23
Single with children	7	6	6	5	6	4
Single male without children	21	21	20	20	21	20
Single female without children	12	12	11	10	11	10
Total benefit units (base=100%)	**1,529**	**3,670**	**2,596**	**2,093**	**2,660**	**2,805**

Table 2.12: Continued

Percentage of benefit units

Government Office Region

Family status	London	South East	South West	England	Wales	Scotland	**Great Britain**
Pensioner couple	6	10	12	9	10	8	**9**
Single male pensioner	4	3	3	3	3	3	**3**
Single female pensioner	10	10	13	11	12	11	**11**
Couple with children	16	19	18	18	17	16	**18**
Couple without children	16	23	21	21	20	20	**21**
Single with children	7	5	5	6	6	6	**6**
Single male without children	25	19	18	21	21	22	**21**
Single female without children	16	11	10	12	11	15	**12**
Total benefit units (base=100%)	**3,348**	**4,113**	**2,527**	**25,341**	**1,639**	**2,595**	**29,575**

Table 2.13: Benefit units by economic status and region

	Government Office Region					
Economic status	North East	North West and Merseyside	Yorkshire and the Humber	East Midlands	West Midlands	Eastern
Self employed	5	5	6	6	6	9
Single or couple, all in full time work	26	30	27	31	31	30
Couple, one in full time work, one in part time work	8	9	9	11	9	10
Couple, one in full time work, one not working	7	7	7	8	8	9
One or more in part time work	9	8	8	7	7	7
Head or spouse aged 60 or over	25	24	24	24	24	24
Head or spouse unemployed	6	5	5	4	4	3
Head or spouse sick or disabled	10	7	6	5	6	4
Others	5	5	6	5	5	4
Total benefit units (base=100%)	**1,529**	**3,670**	**2,596**	**2,093**	**2,660**	**2,805**

Table 2.13: Continued

	Government Office Region						
Economic status	London	South East	South West	England	Wales	Scotland	Great Britain
Self employed	8	8	9	7	6	4	**7**
Single or couple, all in full time work	32	33	26	30	26	29	**30**
Couple, one in full time work, one in part time work	5	10	10	9	8	8	**9**
Couple, one in full time work, one not working	7	8	6	7	7	7	**7**
One or more in part time work	8	8	9	8	6	9	**8**
Head or spouse aged 60 or over	19	22	27	23	28	23	**24**
Head or spouse unemployed	5	3	3	4	4	6	**4**
Head or spouse sick or disabled	6	4	5	6	8	9	**6**
Others	9	4	4	5	7	5	**5**
Total benefit units (base=100%)	**3,348**	**4,113**	**2,527**	**25,341**	**1,639**	**2,595**	**29,575**

DSS, Family Resources Survey Great Britain 1999-2000, © Crown Copyright 2001

Table 2.14: Benefit units by ethnic group of head and region

			Government Office Region			
Ethnic group	North East	North West and Merseyside	Yorkshire and the Humber	East Midlands	West Midlands	Eastern
White	99	95	94	94	94	98
Black	-	1	1	1	2	-
Indian	-	1	1	3	2	-
Pakistani/Bangladeshi	-	3	3	-	1	-
Other	-	1	1	1	1	1
Total benefit units (base=100%)	**1,529**	**3,670**	**2,596**	**2,093**	**2,660**	**2,805**

Table 2.14 Continued

Percentage of benefit units

				Government Office Region			
Ethnic group	London	South East	South West	England	Wales	Scotland	**Great Britain**
White	76	97	99	93	98	99	**94**
Black	9	1	1	2	-	-	**2**
Indian	4	1	-	1	-	0	**1**
Pakistani/Bangladeshi	5	1	-	2	-	-	**2**
Other	6	1	-	2	1	1	**2**
Total benefit units (base=100%)	**3,348**	**4,113**	**2,527**	**25,341**	**1,639**	**2,595**	**29,575**

Table 2.15: Benefit units by age of head and family status

Age		Pensioner couple	Single male pensioner	Single female pensioner	Couple with children	Couple without children	Single with children	Single male without children	Single female without children	Total benefit units
	Family status									
16 to 19		0	0	0	-	-	3	15	17	5
20 to 24		0	0	0	2	3	11	22	26	9
25 to 29		0	0	0	7	8	18	17	14	9
30 to 34		0	0	0	18	7	20	12	8	9
35 to 39		0	0	0	23	5	19	8	5	9
40 to 44		0	0	0	22	6	14	6	6	8
45 to 49		0	0	0	16	10	9	6	6	7
50 to 54		0	0	0	9	20	5	6	9	8
55 to 59		0	0	0	3	20	1	5	9	7
60 to 64		-	0	11	1	19	-	3	0	6
65 to 69		37	25	17	0	0	0	0	0	6
70 to 74		29	24	20	0	0	0	0	0	6
75 to 79		22	24	23	0	0	0	0	0	5
80 to 84		8	14	16	0	0	0	0	0	3
85 or over		4	14	13	0	0	0	0	0	2
Total benefit units (base=100%)		**2,966**	**1,186**	**3,452**	**5,862**	**5,757**	**2,131**	**4,786**	**3,435**	**29,575**

Table 2.16: Benefit units by age of head and region

		Government Office Region				
Age	North East	North West and Merseyside	Yorkshire and the Humber	East Midlands	West Midlands	Eastern
16 to 19	7	6	5	5	6	4
20 to 24	8	10	10	9	9	11
25 to 29	9	9	9	9	9	9
30 to 34	9	9	10	9	9	9
35 to 39	8	9	9	8	8	8
40 to 44	9	8	8	8	7	7
45 to 49	6	8	7	8	7	6
50 to 54	9	7	8	9	8	9
55 to 59	7	6	7	7	7	7
60 to 64	7	6	7	6	7	6
65 to 69	7	6	5	6	6	7
70 to 74	5	6	6	6	5	6
75 to 79	5	5	5	5	6	5
80 to 84	3	2	3	3	3	3
85 or over	2	2	2	2	2	3
Total benefit units (base=100%)	**1,529**	**3,670**	**2,596**	**2,093**	**2,660**	**2,805**

Table 2.16: Continued

		Government Office Region				
Age	London	South East	South West	England	Wales	Scotland	**Great Britain**
16 to 19	4	5	5	5	5	7	**5**
20 to 24	11	9	7	9	10	10	**9**
25 to 29	13	8	8	9	9	8	**9**
30 to 34	11	9	8	9	8	9	**9**
35 to 39	10	9	9	9	7	9	**9**
40 to 44	8	8	8	8	7	8	**8**
45 to 49	7	8	7	7	7	7	**7**
50 to 54	8	9	9	8	8	7	**8**
55 to 59	6	6	7	7	7	8	**7**
60 to 64	4	6	6	6	7	6	**6**
65 to 69	5	7	7	6	6	5	**6**
70 to 74	4	5	7	5	6	6	**6**
75 to 79	4	5	6	5	6	5	**5**
80 to 84	3	3	4	3	4	2	**3**
85 or over	2	2	4	2	2	2	**2**
Total benefit units (base=100%)	**3,348**	**4,113**	**2,527**	**25,341**	**1,639**	**2,595**	**29,575**

DSS, Family Resources Survey Great Britain 1999-2000, © Crown Copyright 2001

Table 2.17 Benefit units by age of head and economic status

Percentage of benefit units

			Economic status		
Age	Self employed	Single or couple, all in full time work	Couple, one in full time work, one in part time work	Couple, one in full time work, one not working	One or more in part time work
16 to 19	1	48	-	-	15
20 to 24	3	51	1	3	10
25 to 29	4	57	5	6	6
30 to 34	9	43	12	10	6
35 to 39	10	37	18	12	7
40 to 44	12	34	19	11	7
45 to 49	13	38	17	10	7
50 to 54	13	31	18	12	9
55 to 59	12	21	12	14	12
60 to 64	7	9	8	11	15
65 to 69	3	1	1	3	9
70 to 74	1	-	-	1	5
75 to 79	-	-	-	-	2
80 to 84	-	0	-	0	1
85 or over	0	0	0	0	-
Total benefit units	**7**	**30**	**9**	**7**	**8**

Table 2.17: Continued

Percentage of benefit units

			Economic status		Total
Age	Head or spouse aged 60 or over	Head or spouse unemployed	Head or spouse sick or disabled	Others	benefit units (base=100%)
16 to 19	0	15	4	17	1,245
20 to 24	0	9	5	19	2,227
25 to 29	0	6	6	9	2,428
30 to 34	0	7	7	6	2,705
35 to 39	-	5	6	4	2,859
40 to 44	-	4	9	3	2,452
45 to 49	-	4	9	1	2,217
50 to 54	-	3	12	2	2,438
55 to 59	2	3	18	6	1,926
60 to 64	52	0	0	0	1,938
65 to 69	84	0	0	0	1,970
70 to 74	93	0	0	0	1,803
75 to 79	97	0	0	0	1,685
80 to 84	99	0	0	0	952
85 or over	100	0	0	0	730
Total benefit units	**24**	**4**	**6**	**5**	**29,575**

DSS, Family Resources Survey Great Britain 1999-2000, © Crown Copyright 2001

Table 2.18: Benefit units by marital status of head and family status

Marital status	Pensioner couple	Single male pensioner	Single female pensioner	Couple with children	Couple without children	Single with children	Single male without children	Single female without children	Total benefit units
Married	98	0	0	87	83	0	0	0	41
Cohabiting	2	0	0	13	17	0	0	0	6
Single	0	22	12	0	0	40	82	74	31
Widowed	0	60	75	0	0	5	2	5	11
Separated	0	4	2	0	0	22	4	5	3
Divorced	0	14	11	0	0	33	11	15	8
Total benefit units (base=100%)	**2,966**	**1,186**	**3,452**	**5,862**	**5,757**	**2,131**	**4,786**	**3,435**	**29,575**

Table 2.19: Benefit units by marital status of head and economic status

Marital status		Economic status			
	Self employed	Single or couple, all in full time work	Couple, one in full time work, one in part time work	Couple, one in full time work, one not working	One or more in part time work
Married	69	26	89	88	38
Cohabiting	10	9	11	12	3
Single	14	52	0	0	36
Widowed	1	2	0	0	5
Separated	2	4	0	0	5
Divorced	5	9	0	0	12
Total benefit units (base=100%)	**2,009**	**7,998**	**2,761**	**2,264**	**2,400**

Table 2.19: Continued

Percentage of benefit units

Marital status		Economic status			Total benefit units
	Head or spouse aged 60 or over	Head or spouse unemployed	Head or spouse sick or disabled	Others	
Married	40	13	23	6	**41**
Cohabiting	1	5	3	1	**6**
Single	9	66	41	71	**31**
Widowed	42	1	6	3	**11**
Separated	2	5	7	9	**3**
Divorced	7	10	19	11	**8**
Total benefit units (base=100%)	**7,691**	**1,149**	**1,760**	**1,543**	**29,575**

Table 2.20: Individuals by sex, age and region

Individuals by age and sex	North East	North West and Merseyside	Yorkshire and the Humber	East Midlands	West Midlands	Eastern
Male						
4 and under	6	6	7	6	7	6
5 to 10	9	8	8	8	8	7
11 to 15	6	7	8	6	7	6
16 to 19	6	7	6	5	6	4
20 to 24	6	6	6	6	6	7
25 to 29	6	6	6	8	7	7
30 to 34	7	7	8	8	8	8
35 to 39	7	8	7	7	7	7
40 to 44	8	7	7	7	6	6
45 to 49	5	7	6	7	7	6
50 to 54	9	6	7	8	7	9
55 to 59	6	6	6	6	6	7
60 to 64	6	5	6	5	6	5
65 to 69	5	4	4	4	5	5
70 to 74	4	4	3	4	3	3
75 to 79	2	3	3	3	3	3
80 to 84	1	1	1	1	1	2
85 or over	1	1	1	1	1	1
Total males (base=100%)	**1,386**	**3,485**	**2,591**	**2,087**	**2,602**	**2,757**
Female						
4 and under	5	5	7	6	6	6
5 to 10	8	8	9	7	7	7
11 to 15	7	7	6	6	6	5
16 to 19	6	5	5	5	5	4
20 to 24	4	6	6	5	5	6
25 to 29	6	6	7	7	6	6
30 to 34	7	8	8	7	7	7
35 to 39	9	7	7	8	7	6
40 to 44	7	7	6	7	7	7
45 to 49	7	7	7	6	7	6
50 to 54	7	6	7	9	7	8
55 to 59	5	6	6	6	6	6
60 to 64	6	6	6	5	5	6
65 to 69	5	5	5	5	5	5
70 to 74	4	5	4	5	4	5
75 to 79	4	4	4	4	4	4
80 to 84	3	2	2	2	2	2
85 or over	2	1	1	2	1	2
Total females (base=100%)	**1,559**	**3,839**	**2,777**	**2,171**	**2,766**	**2,932**

DSS, Family Resources Survey Great Britain 1999-2000, © Crown Copyright 2001

Table 2.20: Continued

Government Office Region

Individuals by age and sex	London	South East	South West	England	Wales	Scotland	Great Britain
Male							
4 and under	8	6	7	7	6	6	6
5 to 10	8	8	8	8	8	9	8
11 to 15	7	6	6	7	6	6	7
16 to 19	6	6	5	6	6	6	6
20 to 24	7	6	5	6	6	6	6
25 to 29	10	6	6	7	8	7	7
30 to 34	10	7	8	8	7	7	8
35 to 39	8	8	8	7	6	8	7
40 to 44	6	7	7	7	7	7	7
45 to 49	6	7	7	6	7	7	7
50 to 54	7	8	8	8	8	7	8
55 to 59	6	5	6	6	6	7	6
60 to 64	3	6	5	5	6	5	5
65 to 69	4	5	5	4	5	4	4
70 to 74	3	3	4	4	4	4	4
75 to 79	3	3	4	3	4	2	3
80 to 84	1	1	2	1	1	1	1
85 or over	1	1	2	1	1	1	1
Total males (base=100%)	**3,074**	**4,089**	**2,429**	**24,500**	**1,536**	**2,323**	**28,359**
Female							
4 and under	7	6	5	6	5	5	6
5 to 10	7	7	8	8	7	6	7
11 to 15	6	7	6	6	6	6	6
16 to 19	5	4	4	5	5	5	5
20 to 24	7	5	5	6	7	6	6
25 to 29	10	6	6	7	5	6	7
30 to 34	8	7	7	7	6	7	7
35 to 39	8	7	7	7	6	8	7
40 to 44	6	6	6	7	6	8	7
45 to 49	6	8	6	7	7	7	7
50 to 54	6	8	7	7	7	6	7
55 to 59	5	5	6	6	6	6	6
60 to 64	4	5	5	5	6	6	5
65 to 69	4	5	6	5	6	5	5
70 to 74	3	4	5	4	5	5	4
75 to 79	3	4	5	4	4	4	4
80 to 84	2	2	3	2	3	2	2
85 or over	2	1	3	2	2	2	2
Total females (base=100%)	**3,284**	**4,357**	**2,667**	**26,352**	**1,714**	**2,585**	**30,651**

Table 2.20: Continued

		Government Office Region				
Individuals by age and sex	North East	North West and Merseyside	Yorkshire and the Humber	East Midlands	West Midlands	Eastern
Total individuals						
4 and under	5	6	7	6	7	6
5 to 10	8	8	9	7	8	7
11 to 15	7	7	7	6	6	6
16 to 19	6	6	5	5	5	4
20 to 24	5	6	6	5	6	6
25 to 29	6	6	7	7	6	6
30 to 34	7	7	8	8	7	7
35 to 39	8	8	7	7	7	7
40 to 44	7	7	6	7	6	7
45 to 49	6	7	6	7	7	6
50 to 54	8	6	7	8	7	9
55 to 59	6	6	6	6	6	6
60 to 64	6	6	6	5	5	6
65 to 69	5	5	4	5	5	5
70 to 74	4	4	4	4	4	4
75 to 79	3	3	3	4	4	4
80 to 84	2	1	1	2	2	2
85 or over	1	1	1	1	1	1
Total individuals (base =100%)	2,945	7,324	5,368	4,258	5,368	5,689

Percentage of individuals

Government Office Region

Individuals by age and sex	London	South East	South West	England	Wales	Scotland	**Great Britain**
Total individuals							
4 and under	8	6	6	6	5	6	**6**
5 to 10	8	8	8	8	8	8	**8**
11 to 15	6	6	6	6	6	6	**6**
16 to 19	5	5	5	5	6	6	**5**
20 to 24	7	6	5	6	6	6	**6**
25 to 29	10	6	6	7	6	6	**7**
30 to 34	9	7	7	8	6	7	**7**
35 to 39	8	8	7	7	6	8	**7**
40 to 44	6	7	6	7	6	8	**7**
45 to 49	6	7	7	7	7	7	**7**
50 to 54	6	8	8	7	7	7	**7**
55 to 59	5	5	6	6	6	6	**6**
60 to 64	4	6	5	5	6	6	**5**
65 to 69	4	5	5	5	5	4	**5**
70 to 74	3	4	5	4	4	4	**4**
75 to 79	3	3	4	3	4	3	**3**
80 to 84	2	2	2	2	2	1	**2**
85 or over	1	1	2	1	1	1	**1**
Total individuals (base =100%)	**6,358**	**8,446**	**5,096**	**50,852**	**3,250**	**4,908**	**59,010**

DSS, Family Resources Survey Great Britain 1999-2000, © Crown Copyright 2001

Chapter 3

Income and benefit receipt

Introduction

The primary function of the FRS is to collect information on the resources of households, that is, income received from all sources including wages and salaries, State benefits, private (occupational and personal) pension schemes and investments. It is crucial for all DSS uses of the survey that this information on income is as accurate as possible. The FRS is also a valuable source of information for analyses of the nature of the support given by the Government to individuals, and in particular, the types and combinations of benefits that households and benefit units receive. It also puts benefits in the context of other sources of income received.

In this chapter, sources of income and receipt of benefits at both household and benefit unit levels are examined.

Contents and points to note when interpreting tables

Tables 3.1 to 3.4 and 3.12 to 3.13 look at the sources of gross weekly income for households and benefit units respectively. These sources include wages and salaries, self employment income, private pensions, State benefits and investment income. For households and benefit units which include an adult over pension age, Retirement Pension (including SERPS and graduated Retirement Pension) and Income Support are shown together in a separate category. This is due to known reporting problems: pensioners do not always recall that they are receiving Income Support and sometimes record total income under Retirement Pension. It is also thought that household surveys underestimate income from both self employment and investment income (impacting particularly on the picture for pensioners), so these figures should be treated with caution. These tables also include a column showing gross average weekly household and benefit unit income respectively.

Tables 3.5 to 3.8 show bands of gross weekly household income. These have been included to allow comparisons with previous reports. Income has been used as a classificatory variable and the tables do not show comparisons of the income distribution across the population. These types of living standard comparisons can only be made following further work, for example, adjusting income for household size and composition, creating a measure of "disposable" income and assessing the impact of housing costs. The DSS statistical series Households Below Average Income (HBAI) provides the most accurate picture of the disposable income distribution in Great Britain.

Tables 3.9 and 3.10 show information on benefit receipt for households, whilst 3.14 to 3.26 provide analyses on a benefit unit basis. Unlike the source of income tables, Retirement Pension is shown separately from Income Support. 70 per cent of all households are in receipt of at least one benefit ("any benefit" category). This apparently high figure is because of the inclusion of Retirement Pension and Child Benefit. In total, 59 per cent of households receive either one or the other.

Tables 3.25 and 3.26 show all benefit units by number of disability benefits received and family and economic status respectively. Note that no account is taken of rules of entitlement to disability benefits.

Table 3.11 shows average weekly housing costs by tenure type and gross weekly household income. Unlike other tables these values are amounts and not percentages.

Table 3.27 looks at receipt of maintenance and separation allowances, showing the amount of maintenance received and the proportion of all single parents and couples with children in the survey who received such payments. Figures include formal and informal money payments from a previous partner as reported by respondents in respect of themselves, their children, or both. This includes payments to individuals via the Child Support Agency (CSA) or the DSS. Recipients of Income Support (IS) whose maintenance is collected by the CSA and then offset against the IS already paid are not included, to avoid any double counting of income.

Table 3.28 analyses pension provision reported by pensioner benefit units.

Tables 3.29 to 3.31 show data on different types of cover from personal insurance policies other than life insurance. For insurance, other than mortgage protection, the FRS asks whether anyone has any policies that cover the items shown in the tables. The tables show households where at least one person holds a policy that covers them for the specific items. It could be that one person holds a single policy that covers more than one item. In such cases, the household would be counted more than once in the table under each type of cover.

Key definitions used
(for a full explanation of all definitions please refer to the Glossary)

- Any benefit
- Economic status
- Family status
- Gross weekly household income
- Gross weekly benefit unit income

- Head of household
- Head of benefit unit
- Income related benefits
- Insurance cover
- Non-income related benefits
- Pensioner benefit unit

Changes to tables between 1998-1999 and 1999-2000

Tables 3.10 and 3.14 – 3.20 include Working Families' Tax Credit (WFTC) with Family Credit (FC). They are counted together as WFTC was introduced in October 1999 to replace FC. Future publications will only show WFTC.

Tables 3.29 – 3.31 include critical illness, an additional type of insurance cover.

Table 3.29 has been changed to show households without children before households with children. This change has been made for consistency with other household composition tables in the publication.

Table 3.1: Components of gross weekly household income by region

Percentage of gross weekly household income

Government Office Region	Wages and salaries	Self employment income	Investments	State Retirement Pension plus any IS	Other pensions	Social Security disability benefits	Other Social Security benefits	Other sources	Gross household income (=100%) (£ per week)
				Source of income					
North East	62	5	2	8	6	6	10	2	370
North West and Merseyside	63	8	3	7	6	3	7	2	440
Yorkshire and the Humber	63	8	3	7	7	3	8	2	410
East Midlands	67	8	3	6	6	3	6	2	450
West Midlands	65	9	3	7	6	3	7	2	450
Eastern	65	11	3	6	7	2	4	2	510
London	66	12	3	4	4	1	7	2	570
South East	68	9	4	5	7	1	4	2	580
South West	58	10	4	8	10	2	6	2	430
England	64	9	3	6	7	2	6	2	480
Wales	57	8	2	8	9	5	8	2	400
Scotland	64	6	3	6	7	4	8	3	420
Great Britain	**64**	**9**	**3**	**6**	**7**	**3**	**6**	**2**	**470**

Table 3.2: Components of gross weekly household income by ethnic group of head

Percentage of gross weekly household income

Ethnic group	Wages and salaries	Self employment income	Investments	State Retirement Pension plus any IS	Other pensions	Social Security disability benefits	Other Social Security benefits	Other sources	Gross household income (=100%) (£ per week)
				Source of income					
White	64	9	3	6	7	3	6	2	470
Black	66	10	-	4	2	2	15	2	390
Indian	64	18	2	2	2	2	9	2	520
Pakistani/Bangladeshi	44	12	1	4	1	4	29	5	350
Other	62	11	3	2	2	1	12	8	460
Total households	**64**	**9**	**3**	**6**	**7**	**3**	**6**	**2**	**470**

Table 3.3: Components of gross weekly household income by age of head

Source of income

Age	Wages and salaries	Self employment income	Investments	State Retirement Pension plus any IS	Other pensions	Social Security disability benefits	Other Social Security benefits	Other sources	Gross household income (=100%) (£ per week)
16 to 24	61	3	1	0	-	1	17	16	310
25 to 34	80	7	1	-	-	1	9	2	500
35 to 44	76	12	2	-	-	1	7	2	600
45 to 54	75	12	2	-	2	2	4	2	650
55 to 59	64	11	4	1	9	4	4	2	540
60 to 64	45	7	6	6	21	7	5	2	400
65 to 74	13	3	8	37	29	4	4	2	290
75 to 84	7	1	9	43	25	6	7	1	220
85 or over	5	-	8	47	20	8	11	1	200
Total households	**64**	**9**	**3**	**6**	**7**	**3**	**6**	**2**	**470**

DSS, Family Resources Survey Great Britain 1999-2000, © Crown Copyright 2001

Table 3.4: Components of gross weekly household income by composition

Percentage of gross weekly household income

Household composition	Wages and salaries	Self employment income	Investments	State Retirement Pension plus any IS
Households without children				
One adult				
adult male over pension age	1	3	11	41
adult female over pension age	3	-	7	49
adult male under pension age	71	12	3	0
adult female under pension age	75	4	2	0
Two adults				
both over pension age	4	2	10	42
one over pension age	39	7	6	14
both under pension age	78	10	3	-
Three or more adults	72	9	2	3
Households with children				
One adult				
one child	43	2	-	-
two children	33	2	-	0
three or more children	16	2	-	0
Two adults				
one child	78	9	2	-
two children	76	14	2	-
three or more children	67	14	1	-
Three or more adults				
one child	76	11	1	1
two children	73	11	1	1
three or more children	68	5	1	2
Total households without children	60	8	4	9
Total households with children	71	11	1	-
Households with one or more adults over pension age	*19*	*4*	*7*	*33*
Households with one or more sick or disabled adults under pension age	*58*	*8*	*2*	*2*
Households with one or more unemployed adults under pension age	*50*	*8*	*2*	*2*

Source of income

Table 3.4: Continued

Household composition	Other pensions	Social Security disability benefits	Other Social Security benefits	Other sources	Gross household income (=100%) (£ per week)
Households without children					
One adult					
adult male over pension age	31	5	7	1	200
adult female over pension age	22	5	12	2	160
adult male under pension age	3	3	7	2	350
adult female under pension age	3	4	10	3	290
Two adults					
both over pension age	35	4	2	1	310
one over pension age	22	7	4	1	390
both under pension age	4	2	2	1	620
Three or more adults	5	3	3	4	740
Households with children					
One adult					
one child	1	2	44	8	230
two children	1	2	52	11	250
three or more children	-	2	69	10	260
Two adults					
one child	2	1	6	2	590
two children	1	1	6	1	700
three or more children	1	2	13	2	610
Three or more adults					
one child	2	2	5	2	730
two children	1	2	7	3	780
three or more children	1	2	18	5	660
Total households without children	10	3	4	2	430
Total households with children	1	1	11	2	580
Households with one or more adults over pension age	*25*	*5*	*5*	*1*	*280*
Households with one or more sick or disabled adults under pension age	*6*	*9*	*13*	*2*	*420*
Households with one or more unemployed adults under pension age	*3*	*3*	*27*	*4*	*320*

DSS, Family Resources Survey Great Britain 1999-2000, © Crown Copyright 2001

Table 3.5 Households by composition and gross weekly household income

Percentage of households

Household composition	Gross weekly household income								
	Under £100 a week	£100 and less than £200	£200 and less than £300	£300 and less than £400	£400 and less than £500	£500 and less than £600	£600 and less than £700	£700 and above	Total households
Households without children									
One adult									
adult male over pension age	8	9	3	2	1	1	1	-	3
adult female over pension age	40	29	10	3	1	1	-	-	11
adult male under pension age	25	11	10	13	9	7	6	4	10
adult female under pension age	10	7	7	6	5	3	2	1	5
Two adults									
both over pension age	1	14	19	12	7	5	3	2	9
one over pension age	2	4	7	8	6	5	3	2	5
both under pension age	6	7	12	19	24	28	31	29	19
Three or more adults	1	1	5	7	11	13	15	21	9
Households with children									
One adult									
one child	2	7	4	2	1	1	-	-	3
two children	1	4	4	2	1	1	-	-	2
three or more children	-	2	4	1	-	-	-	-	1
Two adults									
one child	2	2	4	8	10	10	10	10	7
two children	1	2	5	8	11	14	15	14	8
three or more children	1	1	4	6	6	5	5	5	4
Three or more adults									
one child	-	-	1	1	3	4	6	6	3
two children	-	-	-	1	1	1	2	3	1
three or more children	-	-	-	1	1	1	1	1	1
Total households without children	93	83	74	70	66	62	60	60	71
Total households with children	7	17	26	30	34	38	40	40	29
Households with one or more adults over pension age	*51*	*57*	*42*	*28*	*21*	*16*	*11*	*9*	*31*
Households with one or more sick or disabled adults under pension age	*20*	*23*	*27*	*25*	*23*	*22*	*20*	*17*	*22*
Households with one or more unemployed adults under pension age	*16*	*8*	*7*	*5*	*5*	*4*	*3*	*3*	*6*

Table 3.6: Households by region and gross weekly household income

Government Office Region	Under £100 a week	£100 and less than £200	£200 and less than £300	£300 and less than £400	£400 and less than £500	£500 and less than £600	£600 and less than £700	£700 and above	Total households
				Gross weekly household income					
North East	7	7	6	5	5	4	4	3	5
North West and Merseyside	12	13	14	13	12	12	13	10	12
Yorkshire and the Humber	9	10	9	10	9	10	8	6	9
East Midlands	8	7	7	7	7	7	8	7	7
West Midlands	7	9	9	10	9	10	10	7	9
Eastern	9	8	9	8	10	11	9	11	9
London	11	12	12	11	11	11	13	18	13
South East	10	11	11	12	13	15	15	19	13
South West	10	8	8	9	10	10	8	7	8
England	83	85	84	86	86	89	88	89	86
Wales	6	6	6	6	6	6	4	4	5
Scotland	10	9	10	8	8	6	8	8	8
Great Britain (base=100%)	**1,345**	**5,721**	**4,247**	**2,950**	**2,475**	**2,123**	**1,604**	**4,523**	**24,988**

Table 3.7: Households by ethnic group of head and gross weekly household income

Ethnic group	Under £100 a week	£100 and less than £200	£200 and less than £300	£300 and less than £400	£400 and less than £500	£500 and less than £600	£600 and less than £700	£700 and above	Total households
				Gross weekly household income					
White	95	95	94	94	94	95	95	96	95
Black	2	2	2	2	2	2	1	1	2
Indian	-	1	1	1	1	1	2	1	1
Pakistani/Bangladeshi	1	1	2	2	1	-	1	-	1
Other	1	1	2	1	1	1	1	1	1
Total households (base=100%)	**1,345**	**5,721**	**4,247**	**2,950**	**2,475**	**2,123**	**1,604**	**4,523**	**24,988**

Table 3.8: Households by access to consumer durables and gross weekly household income

Consumer durables	Under £100 a week	£100 and less than £200	£200 and less than £300	£300 and less than £400	£400 and less than £500	£500 and less than £600	£600 and less than £700	£700 and above	Total households
				Gross weekly household income					
Satellite dish/cable	13	17	26	31	36	40	42	42	30
Video recorder	59	68	83	91	94	95	97	97	85
Deep Freeze or Fridge/freezer	79	86	92	96	96	97	97	98	93
Washing machine	76	81	90	94	96	98	99	99	91
Tumble dryer	29	33	45	52	57	60	65	70	51
Dishwasher	8	7	12	17	24	29	35	54	24
Microwave	61	68	79	83	86	88	91	90	80
Telephone	88	90	95	97	98	99	99	100	96
Compact disc player	39	43	62	76	86	88	91	95	71
Home computer	15	11	20	33	45	51	58	71	37
Cars/ light vans	34	35	60	79	88	92	93	97	70
Central heating	78	84	87	89	91	91	94	97	89
Television	96	97	99	99	99	99	99	99	98
Total households (base=100%)	1,345	5,721	4,247	2,950	2,475	2,123	1,604	4,523	24,988

Table 3.9: Households by composition and percentage of gross weekly household income from benefits

Household composition	Percentage of income from benefits				Total households (base=100%)
	On no benefits	On any benefit	50% or more from benefit	50% or more from income related benefits	
Households without children					
One adult					
adult male over pension age	-	100	71	4	1,019
adult female over pension age	-	100	78	8	2,869
adult male under pension age	67	33	28	20	1,963
adult female under pension age	63	37	27	17	1,400
Two adults					
both over pension age	-	100	62	-	2,561
one over pension age	8	92	31	5	1,178
both under pension age	79	21	9	4	4,340
Three or more adults	55	45	11	3	1,656
Households with children					
One adult					
one child	1	99	61	52	807
two children	1	99	69	61	663
three or more children	-	100	84	71	364
Two adults					
one child	2	98	11	6	1,880
two children	1	99	9	6	2,375
three or more children	1	99	21	11	1,070
Three or more adults					
one child	2	98	9	5	512
two children	2	98	13	7	224
three or more children	4	96	31	16	107
Total households without children	42	58	35	7	16,986
Total households with children	1	99	24	17	8,002
Total households	30	70	32	10	24,988
Households with one or more adults over pension age	*2*	*98*	*61*	*4*	8,225
Households with one or more sick or disabled adults under pension age	*23*	*77*	*41*	*20*	5,228
Households with one or more unemployed adults under pension age	*15*	*85*	*55*	*42*	1,309

DSS, Family Resources Survey Great Britain 1999-2000, © Crown Copyright 2001

Table 3.10: Households by benefit receipt and region

Percentage of households

Benefit received		Government Office Region				
	North East	North West and Merseyside	Yorkshire and the Humber	East Midlands	West Midlands	Eastern
Family Credit/Working Families' Tax Credit	3	4	4	3	3	2
Income Support	18	14	12	11	14	9
Housing Benefit	27	17	20	14	17	13
Council Tax Benefit	35	24	26	19	22	18
Retirement Pension	30	31	29	29	31	31
Widow's Benefits	1	1	1	1	1	1
Jobseeker's Allowance	6	4	5	3	4	3
Incapacity Benefit	12	8	7	5	5	3
Severe Disablement Allowance	1	1	1	1	1	1
Attendance Allowance	4	4	3	3	5	3
Invalid Care Allowance	2	1	2	2	2	1
Disability Living Allowance (care component)	9	6	6	6	6	5
Disability Living Allowance (mobility component)	10	8	7	6	6	4
Industrial Injuries Disablement Benefit	3	1	1	1	1	1
War Disablement Pension or War Widow's Pension	1	1	1	1	1	1
Child Benefit	28	31	30	28	29	27
On any income related benefit	40	30	31	24	27	21
On any non-income related benefit	71	70	68	64	68	63
On any benefit	79	74	72	68	71	67
No benefits	21	26	28	32	29	33
Total households (base = 100%)	**1,284**	**3,064**	**2,242**	**1,796**	**2,234**	**2,411**

Table 3.10: Continued

Government Office Region

Benefit received	London	South East	South West	England	Wales	Scotland	**Great Britain**
Family Credit/Working Families' Tax Credit	2	2	3	3	3	3	**3**
Income Support	17	8	11	12	14	15	**13**
Housing Benefit	23	11	14	17	18	24	**18**
Council Tax Benefit	26	13	19	22	24	29	**22**
Retirement Pension	25	30	34	30	33	29	**30**
Widow's Benefits	1	1	1	1	1	2	**1**
Jobseeker's Allowance	4	2	3	4	5	5	**4**
Incapacity Benefit	3	4	5	5	10	9	**6**
Severe Disablement Allowance	1	1	1	1	1	1	**1**
Attendance Allowance	3	2	4	3	5	4	**3**
Invalid Care Allowance	1	1	1	1	2	2	**2**
Disability Living Allowance (care component)	4	3	4	5	9	6	**5**
Disability Living Allowance (mobility component)	3	3	4	5	10	7	**6**
Industrial Injuries Disablement Benefit	-	1	1	1	2	1	**1**
War Disablement Pension or War Widow's Pension	1	1	1	1	1	1	**1**
Child Benefit	30	29	27	29	29	27	**29**
On any income related benefit	30	17	25	26	30	34	**27**
On any non-income related benefit	59	63	66	65	71	66	**66**
On any benefit	65	66	70	69	76	72	**70**
No benefits	35	34	30	31	24	28	**30**
Total households (base = 100%)	**2,661**	**3,529**	**2,226**	**21,447**	**1,358**	**2,183**	**24,988**

DSS, Family Resources Survey Great Britain 1999-2000, © Crown Copyright 2001

Table 3.11: Average weekly housing costs by tenure of dwelling and gross weekly household income

Average weekly housing costs (£ per week)

Tenure of dwelling	Under £100 a week	£100 and less than £200	£200 and less than £300	£300 and less than £400	£400 and less than £500	£500 and less than £600	£600 and less than £700	£700 and above	Total households
Rented accommodation									
Rented from:									
Council	40	46	49	49	49	52	53	55	**47**
Housing Association	54	55	63	73	70	75	71	94	**62**
All social rented sector tenants	43	48	52	56	53	58	57	66	**51**
Rented privately									
Unfurnished	41	53	63	64	60	61	80	112	**65**
Furnished	52	68	87	95	115	129	127	163	**101**
All rented privately	46	60	74	78	86	86	106	141	**82**
Owner occupiers									
Owned outright	7	8	9	9	9	9	9	12	**9**
Buying with mortgage	50	38	42	48	51	56	62	85	**63**
All owners	17	15	22	31	37	44	50	71	**41**
Total households	**28**	**36**	**39**	**41**	**43**	**49**	**55**	**76**	**47**

Table 3.12: Components of gross weekly benefit unit income by family status

Percentage of gross weekly benefit unit income

Family status	Wages and salaries	Self employment income	Investments	State Retirement Pension plus any IS	Other pensions	Social Security disability benefits	Other Social Security benefits	Other sources	Gross benefit unit income (=100%) (£ per week)
Pensioner couple	6	3	9	40	33	4	2	2	**310**
Single male pensioner	1	2	11	42	30	5	7	1	**190**
Single female pensioner	3	-	7	50	21	6	12	2	**160**
Couple with children	76	13	2	-	1	1	6	1	**640**
Couple without children	74	10	3	1	7	3	1	1	**590**
Single with children	36	2	-	0	1	2	50	9	**240**
Single male without children	75	9	2	0	2	2	6	3	**260**
Single female without children	78	3	1	0	2	3	7	6	**210**
Total benefit units	**64**	**9**	**3**	**6**	**7**	**3**	**6**	**2**	**380**

Table 3.13: Components of gross weekly benefit unit income by economic status

Economic status	Source of income			
	Wages and salaries	Self employment income	Investments	State Retirement Pension plus any IS
Self employed	20	70	3	1
Single or couple, all in full time work	96	-	1	-
Couple, one in full time work, one in part time work	90	3	2	-
Couple, one in full time work, one not working	84	-	3	1
One or more in part time work	39	11	5	6
Head or spouse aged 60 or over	-	0	9	42
Head or spouse unemployed	-	0	3	0
Head or spouse sick or disabled	1	0	2	-
Others	1	0	6	0
Total benefit units	**64**	**9**	**3**	**6**

Table 3.13: Continued

Percentage of gross weekly benefit unit income

Family status	Source of income				Gross benefit unit income (=100%) (£ per week)
	Other pensions	Social Security disability benefits	Other Social Security benefits	Other sources	
Self employed	2	-	2	2	**630**
Single or couple, all in full time work	1	-	1	1	**490**
Couple, one in full time work, one in part time work	2	-	2	1	**640**
Couple, one in full time work, one not working	4	2	4	1	**570**
One or more in part time work	18	3	12	6	**270**
Head or spouse aged 60 or over	32	7	8	2	**210**
Head or spouse unemployed	3	4	82	8	**90**
Head or spouse sick or disabled	8	34	51	4	**170**
Others	10	2	53	29	**130**
Total benefit units	**7**	**3**	**6**	**2**	**380**

DSS, Family Resources Survey Great Britain 1999-2000, © Crown Copyright 2001

Table 3.14: Benefit units by benefit receipt and region

Government Office Region

Benefit received	North East	North West and Merseyside	Yorkshire and the Humber	East Midlands	West Midlands	Eastern
Family Credit/Working Families' Tax Credit	2	3	3	2	3	2
Income Support	15	12	11	9	11	7
Housing Benefit	21	14	16	12	13	11
Council Tax Benefit	28	19	21	16	17	14
Retirement Pension	25	25	24	24	25	26
Widow's Benefits	1	1	1	1	1	1
Jobseeker's Allowance	5	4	4	3	3	3
Incapacity Benefit	9	6	5	4	4	3
Severe Disablement Allowance	1	1	1	1	1	1
Attendance Allowance	3	3	2	3	4	2
Invalid Care Allowance	2	1	2	2	1	1
Disability Living Allowance (care component)	7	5	5	5	5	4
Disability Living Allowance (mobility component)	8	6	6	5	5	4
Industrial Injuries Disablement Benefit	2	1	1	1	1	-
War Disablement Pension or War Widow's Pension	1	1	1	1	-	1
Child Benefit	23	25	25	23	23	22
On any income related benefit	35	25	27	20	23	18
On any non-income related benefit	59	57	57	54	56	53
On any benefit	67	62	62	58	60	56
No benefits	33	38	38	42	40	44
Total benefit units (base = 100%)	**1,529**	**3,670**	**2,596**	**2,093**	**2,660**	**2,805**

Government Office Region

Benefit received	London	South East	South West	England	Wales	Scotland	Great Britain
Family Credit/Working Families' Tax Credit	1	1	2	2	3	2	2
Income Support	13	7	10	10	11	13	11
Housing Benefit	18	9	12	14	14	20	14
Council Tax Benefit	20	11	16	17	19	23	18
Retirement Pension	19	24	29	24	27	23	24
Widow's Benefits	1	1	1	1	1	1	1
Jobseeker's Allowance	3	2	2	3	4	4	3
Incapacity Benefit	3	3	4	4	8	7	5
Severe Disablement Allowance	1	1	1	1	1	1	1
Attendance Allowance	2	1	3	3	4	3	3
Invalid Care Allowance	1	1	1	1	2	2	1
Disability Living Allowance (care component)	3	3	4	4	7	5	4
Disability Living Allowance (mobility component)	3	3	4	4	8	6	5
Industrial Injuries Disablement Benefit	-	-	1	1	1	1	1
War Disablement Pension or War Widow's Pension	-	1	1	1	1	1	1
Child Benefit	23	23	23	23	23	22	23
On any income related benefit	25	15	21	23	25	29	23
On any non-income related benefit	47	53	58	54	60	55	55
On any benefit	53	55	62	59	64	62	59
No benefits	47	45	38	41	36	38	41
Total benefit units (base = 100%)	3,348	4,113	2,527	25,341	1,639	2,595	29,575

DSS, Family Resources Survey Great Britain 1999-2000, © Crown Copyright 2001

Table 3.15: Benefit units by benefit receipt and family status

				Family status					
Benefit received	Pensioner couple	Single male pensioner	Single female pensioner	Couple with children	Couple without children	Single with children	Single male without children	Single female without children	Total benefit units
Family Credit/Working Families' Tax Credit	0	0	0	7	0	19	0	-	2
Income Support	6	12	24	5	4	54	7	8	11
Housing Benefit	10	29	29	8	5	57	11	10	14
Council Tax Benefit	17	35	42	11	7	62	11	12	18
Retirement Pension	99	97	96	-	9	0	0	0	24
Widow's Benefits	-	0	1	-	-	3	0	4	1
Jobseeker's Allowance	0	0	0	3	2	1	9	4	3
Incapacity Benefit	1	1	-	4	11	2	5	4	5
Severe Disablement Allowance	1	-	-	-	1	-	1	1	1
Attendance Allowance	10	10	14	-	-	0	0	-	3
Invalid Care Allowance	1	0	-	2	2	3	1	1	1
Disability Living Allowance (care component)	6	3	3	4	6	5	3	4	4
Disability Living Allowance (mobility component)	9	4	4	4	7	4	3	4	5
Industrial Injuries Disablement Benefit	2	1	-	1	1	-	-	-	1
War Disablement Pension or War Widow's Pension	3	4	1	-	-	0	-	-	1
Child Benefit	1	-	-	98	-	98	-	-	23
On any income related benefit	19	40	45	16	9	79	20	18	23
On any non-income related benefit	99	99	98	98	25	98	10	14	55
On any benefit	100	99	99	98	28	99	23	23	59
No benefits	-	1	1	2	72	1	77	77	41
Total benefit units (base =100%)	2,966	1,186	3,452	5,862	5,757	2,131	4,786	3,435	29,575

Percentage of benefit units

Economic status

Benefit received	Self employed	Single or couple, all in full time work	Couple, one in full time work, one in part time work	Couple, one in full time work, one not working	One or more in part time work
Family Credit/Working Families' Tax Credit	2	1	1	7	13
Income Support	-	-	0	-	5
Housing Benefit	1	1	1	3	16
Council Tax Benefit	2	2	1	4	19
Retirement Pension	5	1	3	8	18
Widow's Benefits	-	1	-	-	2
Jobseeker's Allowance	-	-	-	3	3
Incapacity Benefit	2	-	0	11	7
Severe Disablement Allowance	-	-	0	1	-
Attendance Allowance	0	-	-	-	-
Invalid Care Allowance	-	-	1	2	1
Disability Living Allowance (care component)	2	-	1	6	4
Disability Living Allowance (mobility component)	1	-	1	7	4
Industrial Injuries Disablement Benefit	1	-	-	2	1
War Disablement Pension or War Widow's Pension	-	-	-	1	-
Child Benefit	40	15	61	51	27
On any income related benefit	4	3	3	11	28
On any non-income related benefit	47	17	65	73	53
On any benefit	48	19	66	74	59
No benefits	52	81	34	26	41
Total benefit units (base =100%)	**2,009**	**7,998**	**2,761**	**2,264**	**2,400**

Table 3.16: Continued

Economic status

Benefit received	Head or spouse aged 60 or over	Head or spouse unemployed	Head or spouse sick or disabled	Others	Total benefit units
Family Credit/Working Families' Tax Credit	0	I	-	I	2
Income Support	17	12	58	40	11
Housing Benefit	24	41	52	34	14
Council Tax Benefit	34	44	60	37	18
Retirement Pension	91	0	-	0	24
Widow's Benefits	-	I	3	2	1
Jobseeker's Allowance	-	59	0	0	3
Incapacity Benefit	4	3	37	I	5
Severe Disablement Allowance	I	I	8	-	1
Attendance Allowance	12	0	0	0	3
Invalid Care Allowance	I	I	6	5	1
Disability Living Allowance (care component)	6	2	27	3	4
Disability Living Allowance (mobility component)	8	2	28	I	5
Industrial Injuries Disablement Benefit	I	-	2	0	1
War Disablement Pension or War Widow's Pension	2	0	-	-	1
Child Benefit	I	20	26	38	23
On any income related benefit	37	71	75	44	23
On any non-income related benefit	96	30	78	44	55
On any benefit	98	77	92	48	59
No benefits	2	23	8	52	41
Total benefit units (base = 100%)	**7,691**	**1,149**	**1,760**	**1,543**	**29,575**

Table 3.17: Benefit units by benefit receipt and ethnic group of head

Percentage of benefit units

Benefit received	White	Black	Indian	Pakistani/ Bangladeshi	Other	Total benefit units
Family Credit/Working Families' Tax Credit	2	4	4	8	3	2
Income Support	10	19	14	22	16	11
Housing Benefit	14	28	9	19	19	14
Council Tax Benefit	18	29	15	29	20	18
Retirement Pension	25	13	8	6	6	24
Widow's Benefits	1	-	1	2	1	1
Jobseeker's Allowance	3	8	4	9	4	3
Incapacity Benefit	5	2	4	3	2	5
Severe Disablement Allowance	1	-	1	-	1	1
Attendance Allowance	3	1	1	1	1	3
Invalid Care Allowance	1	1	1	4	1	1
Disability Living Allowance (care component)	4	3	3	6	2	4
Disability Living Allowance (mobility component)	5	4	3	5	3	5
Industrial Injuries Disablement Benefit	1	-	0	-	-	1
War Disablement Pension or War Widow's Pension	1	-	0	0	0	1
Child Benefit	22	30	34	42	27	23
On any income related benefit	23	37	24	44	27	23
On any non-income related benefit	55	47	47	52	39	55
On any benefit	59	60	55	62	49	59
No benefits	41	40	45	38	51	41
Total benefit units (base=100%)	**27,913**	**526**	**335**	**390**	**411**	**29,575**

DSS, Family Resources Survey Great Britain 1999-2000, © Crown Copyright 2001

Table 3.18: Benefit units by benefit receipt and age of head

Age

Benefit received	16 to 24	25 to 34	35 to 44	45 to 54	55 to 59	60 to 64	65 to 74	75 to 84	85 or over	Total benefit units
Family Credit/Working Families' Tax Credit	1	5	6	2	-	-	0	0	0	**2**
Income Support	7	11	10	8	9	14	11	15	29	**11**
Housing Benefit	8	16	14	10	11	14	18	24	28	**14**
Council Tax Benefit	7	16	17	13	16	21	26	36	44	**18**
Retirement Pension	0	0	-	1	5	42	98	98	98	**24**
Widow's Benefits	-	-	-	2	5	2	-	-	0	**1**
Jobseeker's Allowance	6	5	4	3	3	1	0	0	0	**3**
Incapacity Benefit	-	2	4	9	16	17	1	-	0	**5**
Severe Disablement Allowance	1	1	1	1	2	2	1	-	-	**1**
Attendance Allowance	0	0	-	-	-	-	5	17	34	**3**
Invalid Care Allowance	-	1	2	2	2	3	-	-	-	**1**
Disability Living Allowance (care component)	1	3	5	5	7	11	6	2	2	**4**
Disability Living Allowance (mobility component)	1	2	4	6	8	12	9	3	-	**5**
Industrial Injuries Disablement Benefit	0	-	1	1	1	2	2	1	-	**1**
War Disablement Pension or War Widow's Pension	-	-	-	-	-	1	1	5	3	**1**
Child Benefit	7	35	59	32	7	3	1	-	0	**23**
On any income related benefit	15	24	23	17	19	23	28	39	49	**23**
On any non-income related benefit	11	39	64	46	37	64	99	99	99	**55**
On any benefit	18	46	69	51	43	69	99	100	100	**59**
No benefits	82	54	31	49	57	31	1	-	-	**41**
Total benefit units (base=100%)	**3,472**	**5,133**	**5,311**	**4,655**	**1,926**	**1,938**	**3,773**	**2,637**	**730**	**29,575**

Table 3.19: Benefit units by benefit receipt and number of children

| | Number of children | | | | | | | |
| | Two parent families | | | | One parent families | | | |
Benefit received	One	Two	Three or more	**All two parent families**	One	Two	Three or more	**All one parent families**
Family Credit/Working Families' Tax Credit	4	5	14	**7**	21	19	15	**19**
Income Support	4	4	8	**5**	47	55	71	**54**
Housing Benefit	7	7	14	**8**	51	59	74	**57**
Council Tax Benefit	9	9	19	**11**	54	66	77	**62**
Retirement Pension	-	0	0	**-**	0	0	0	**0**
Widow's Benefits	-	-	-	**-**	3	2	3	**3**
Jobseeker's Allowance	2	3	5	**3**	1	1	1	**1**
Incapacity Benefit	5	3	5	**4**	3	2	1	**2**
Severe Disablement Allowance	-	-	-	**-**	-	-	1	**-**
Attendance Allowance	-	0	0	**-**	0	0	0	**0**
Invalid Care Allowance	1	2	4	**2**	2	2	7	**3**
Disability Living Allowance (care component)	3	4	6	**4**	4	5	10	**5**
Disability Living Allowance (mobility component)	4	3	5	**4**	3	3	7	**4**
Industrial Injuries Disablement Benefit	1	1	-	**1**	-	-	-	**-**
War Disablement Pension or War Widow's Pension	-	-	-	**-**	0	0	0	**0**
Child Benefit	96	99	98	**98**	97	99	99	**98**
On any income related benefit	13	13	29	**16**	73	80	90	**79**
On any non-income related benefit	97	99	98	**98**	98	99	99	**98**
On any benefit	97	99	99	**98**	99	99	100	**99**
No benefits	3	1	1	**2**	1	1	-	**1**
Total benefit units (base = 100%)	**2,209**	**2,517**	**1,136**	**5,862**	**1,015**	**724**	**392**	**2,131**

Table 3.20: Benefit units by benefit receipt and tenure type

Percentage of benefit units

Benefit received	Rented — From Council	Rented — From Housing Association	Rented — Privately unfurnished	Owner occupiers — Privately furnished	Owner occupiers — Owned outright	Owner occupiers — Buying with mortgage	Total benefit units
Family Credit/Working Families' Tax Credit	5	5	4	2	-	2	2
Income Support	31	33	14	12	5	3	11
Housing Benefit	54	57	25	20	-	-	14
Council Tax Benefit	53	54	27	17	10	4	18
Retirement Pension	31	32	23	3	52	5	24
Widow's Benefits	1	1	1	-	2	-	1
Jobseeker's Allowance	7	7	6	5	1	2	3
Incapacity Benefit	8	8	4	3	5	3	5
Severe Disablement Allowance	2	2	1	-	1	1	1
Attendance Allowance	5	5	3	1	4	-	3
Invalid Care Allowance	3	2	1	-	1	1	1
Disability Living Allowance (care component)	9	9	4	2	4	3	4
Disability Living Allowance (mobility component)	9	10	4	2	5	3	5
Industrial Injuries Disablement Benefit	1	1	1	-	1	1	1
War Disablement Pension or War Widow's Pension	1	1	1	-	1	-	1
Child Benefit	26	28	24	11	6	34	23
On any income related benefit	63	63	33	24	13	8	23
On any non-income related benefit	70	72	52	19	66	44	55
On any benefit	80	81	60	29	68	46	59
No benefits	20	19	40	71	32	54	41
Total benefit units (base=100%)	**5,098**	**1,537**	**1,569**	**1,431**	**8,160**	**11,780**	**29,575**

Table 3.21: Benefit units by family status and number of benefits received

Percentage of benefit units

			Number of benefits received				
Family status	None	One	Two	Three	Four	Five or more	Total benefit units (base =100%)
Pensioner couple	-	6	60	15	10	8	**2,966**
Single male pensioner	1	51	16	18	10	4	**1,186**
Single female pensioner	1	47	15	17	15	6	**3,452**
Couple with children	2	76	9	4	6	4	**5,862**
Couple without children	72	14	5	4	2	3	**5,757**
Single with children	1	18	17	10	45	9	**2,131**
Single male without children	77	8	4	7	2	1	**4,786**
Single female without children	77	9	5	6	3	2	**3,435**
Total benefit units	**41**	**27**	**13**	**8**	**8**	**4**	**29,575**

Table 3.22: Benefit units by economic status and number of benefits received

Percentage of benefit units

			Number of benefits received				
Economic status	None	One	Two	Three	Four	Five or more	Total benefit units (base =100%)
Self employed	52	41	5	1	1	-	**2,009**
Single or couple, all in full time work	81	16	2	1	-	-	**7,998**
Couple, one in full time work, one in part time work	34	61	4	1	-	-	**2,761**
Couple, one in full time work, one not working	26	49	16	6	3	1	**2,264**
One or more in part time work	41	22	18	8	9	2	**2,400**
Head or spouse aged 60 or over	2	30	30	17	13	7	**7,691**
Head or spouse unemployed	23	26	10	23	14	3	**1,149**
Head or spouse sick or disabled	8	12	12	23	24	20	**1,760**
Others	52	6	6	6	26	5	**1,543**
Total benefit units	**41**	**27**	**13**	**8**	**8**	**4**	**29,575**

Table 3.23: Benefit units by family status and combinations of benefits received

			Benefits received			
Family status	On no benefits	Only Child Benefit	Only non-income related benefits	Only income related benefits	Income related and non-income related benefits	Total benefit units (base =100%)
Pensioner couple	-	-	81	-	18	2,966
Single male pensioner	1	0	59	1	39	1,186
Single female pensioner	1	0	54	1	45	3,452
Couple with children	2	76	7	-	16	5,862
Couple without children	72	-	19	3	6	5,757
Single with children	1	17	3	1	78	2,131
Single male without children	77	-	3	13	7	4,786
Single female without children	77	-	6	10	8	3,435
Total benefit units	**41**	**14**	**22**	**5**	**19**	**29,575**

Table 3.24: Benefit units by economic status and combinations of benefits received

Percentage of benefit units

			Benefits received			
Economic status	On no benefits	Only Child Benefit	Only non-income related benefits	Only income related benefits	Income related and non-income related benefits	Total benefit units (base =100%)
Self employed	52	36	9	1	3	2,009
Single or couple, all in full time work	81	13	3	2	2	7,998
Couple, one in full time work, one in part time work	34	57	6	-	2	2,761
Couple, one in full time work, one not working	26	35	28	1	10	2,264
One or more in part time work	41	7	25	6	22	2,400
Head or spouse aged 60 or over	2	-	61	2	35	7,691
Head or spouse unemployed	23	1	4	47	24	1,149
Head or spouse sick or disabled	8	1	16	14	62	1,760
Others	52	1	3	4	39	1,543
Total benefit units	**41**	**14**	**22**	**5**	**19**	**29,575**

Table 3.25: Benefit units by family status and number of disability benefits received

| | Number of disability benefits received | | | | Total benefit units |
Family status	None	One	Two	Three or more	(base =100%)
Pensioner couple	76	16	6	2	**2,966**
Single male pensioner	80	16	3	-	**1,186**
Single female pensioner	80	17	2	-	**3,452**
Couple with children	91	5	2	1	**5,862**
Couple without children	84	8	4	4	**5,757**
Single with children	92	5	3	-	**2,131**
Single male without children	92	5	2	1	**4,786**
Single female without children	92	5	2	1	**3,435**
Total benefit units	**87**	**8**	**3**	**2**	**29,575**

Table 3.26: Benefit units by economic status and number of disability benefits received

Percentage of benefit units

| | Number of disability benefits received | | | | Total benefit units |
Economic status	None	One	Two	Three or more	(base =100%)
Self employed	96	2	1	-	**2,009**
Single or couple, all in full time work	99	1	-	-	**7,998**
Couple, one in full time work, one in part time work	98	1	1	0	**2,761**
Couple, one in full time work, one not working	83	11	4	3	**2,264**
One or more in part time work	89	7	2	2	**2,400**
Head or spouse aged 60 or over	75	18	5	2	**7,691**
Head or spouse unemployed	95	3	2	1	**1,149**
Head or spouse sick or disabled	38	32	17	12	**1,760**
Others	97	2	1	-	**1,543**
Total benefit units	**87**	**8**	**3**	**2**	**29,575**

DSS, Family Resources Survey Great Britain 1999-2000, © Crown Copyright 2001

Table 3.27: Benefit units with children by weekly amount of maintenance received and number of dependent children

Percentage of benefit units

| Amount of maintenance | Number of children | | | |
	One	Two	Three or more	Total
Couples				
None received	97	97	94	**96**
Received maintenance	3	3	6	**4**
Of which:				
Less than £25	42	31	32	**35**
£25 but less than £50	41	33	30	**34**
£50 but less than £75	15	28	21	**21**
£75 but less than £100	1	2	11	**5**
£100 or more	1	6	5	**4**
Total couples with maintenance (base=100%)	**72**	**83**	**74**	**229**
Single parents				
None received	81	74	82	**79**
Received maintenance	19	26	18	**21**
Of which:				
Less than £25	30	27	29	**29**
£25 but less than £50	37	27	28	**32**
£50 but less than £75	17	20	14	**17**
£75 but less than £100	7	10	8	**8**
£100 or more	9	16	21	**14**
Total single parents with maintenance (base=100%)	**196**	**191**	**72**	**459**

Table 3.28: Pensioner benefit units by pension provision and age of head

Percentage of benefit units

Pension provision	Age						Total pensioner benefit units
	60 to 64	65 to 69	70 to 74	75 to 79	80 to 84	85 or over	
Pensioner couples							
State Retirement Pension/IS only	.	19	21	22	24	38	**22**
Employee pensions only	.	-	-	0	0	0	**-**
Incapacity Benefit only	.	-	-	0	0	0	**-**
Retirement Pension and employees pension	.	61	62	67	67	57	**63**
Retirement Pension and personal pension	.	8	7	5	4	2	**6**
Incapacity Benefit and employees pension	.	-	0	0	0	0	**-**
Other pension combinations	.	10	9	6	6	3	**8**
No pension	.	1	-	0	0	0	**-**
Total pensioner couples (base=100%)	**5**	**1,100**	**860**	**641**	**247**	**113**	**2,966**
Single male pensioners							
State Retirement Pension/IS only	0	40	32	34	32	40	**36**
Employee pensions only	0	1	0	0	0	0	**-**
Incapacity Benefit only	0	0	0	0	0	0	**0**
Retirement Pension and employees pension	0	46	54	59	59	50	**53**
Retirement Pension and personal pension	0	3	5	2	3	5	**4**
Incapacity Benefit and employees pension	0	3	1	0	0	0	**1**
Other pension combinations	0	6	7	5	6	4	**6**
No pension	0	-	1	0	1	1	**1**
Total single male pensioners (base=100%)	**0**	**294**	**276**	**278**	**176**	**162**	**1,186**

DSS, Family Resources Survey Great Britain 1999–2000, © Crown Copyright 2001

Table 3.28: Continued

Pension provision	60 to 64	65 to 69	70 to 74	75 to 79	80 to 84	85 or over	Total pensioner benefit units
Single female pensioners							
State Retirement Pension/IS only	46	44	45	42	52	63	**48**
Employee pensions only	I	-	-	-	0	0	**-**
Incapacity Benefit only	0	0	0	0	0	0	**0**
Retirement Pension and employees pension	26	21	20	20	15	II	**19**
Retirement Pension and personal pension	4	2	2	I	I	0	**I**
Incapacity Benefit and employees pension	0	0	0	0	0	0	**0**
Other pension combinations	22	33	33	36	31	25	**31**
No pension	I	-	I	-	I	I	**I**
Total single female pensioners (base=100%)	**459**	**576**	**667**	**766**	**529**	**455**	**3,452**
Total pensioners							
State Retirement Pension/IS only	45	30	32	33	42	55	**36**
Employee pensions only	I	I	-	-	0	0	**-**
Incapacity Benefit only	-	-	-	0	0	0	**-**
Retirement Pension and employees pension	26	47	45	44	35	26	**41**
Retirement Pension and personal pension	4	5	5	2	2	I	**4**
Incapacity Benefit and employees pension	0	I	-	0	0	0	**-**
Other pension combinations	22	17	18	20	21	17	**19**
No pension	I	I	-	-	I	I	**I**
Total pensioner benefit units (base=100%)	**464**	**1,970**	**1,803**	**1,685**	**952**	**730**	**7,604**

Table 3.29: Households by insurance cover and household composition

Insurance cover	Households without children				Households with children		
	One male adult	One female adult	Two adults	Three or more adults	One adult	Two adults	Three or more adults
Mortgage protection	14	6	15	17	8	29	26
Personal accident	11	5	15	15	5	19	19
Private medical insurance	13	9	21	21	5	23	20
Permanent health insurance	3	2	4	4	1	6	4
Critical illness	4	2	5	3	2	10	7
Friendly society sickness insurance	1	1	3	2	1	3	3
Nursing home or long term care	-	-	1	-	-	-	-
Any other sickness insurance	2	1	2	2	1	3	2
Redundancy policy	1	1	1	1	1	2	2
Total households (base=100%)	**2,982**	**4,269**	**8,079**	**1,656**	**1,834**	**5,325**	**843**

Table 3.29: Continued

Insurance cover	Households with one or more adults over pension age	Households with one or more sick or disabled adults under pension age	Households with one or more unemployed adults under pension age	Total households
Mortgage protection	2	13	12	16
Personal accident	7	12	9	13
Private medical insurance	10	14	9	17
Permanent health insurance	1	3	2	4
Critical illness	1	3	2	5
Friendly society sickness insurance	2	2	1	2
Nursing home or long term care	-	-	-	-
Any other sickness insurance	1	2	1	2
Redundancy policy	-	1	1	1
Total households (base=100%)	**8,225**	**5,228**	**1,309**	**24,988**

Table 3.30: Households by insurance cover and region

Percentage of households

			Government Office Region			
Insurance cover	North East	North West and Merseyside	Yorkshire and the Humber	East Midlands	West Midlands	Eastern
Mortgage protection	14	16	15	18	18	18
Personal accident	8	11	11	15	14	14
Private medical insurance	8	15	16	14	17	21
Permanent health insurance	2	3	3	3	3	4
Critical illness	3	5	4	6	4	5
Friendly society sickness insurance	1	3	5	2	3	2
Nursing home or long term care	-	-	-	-	-	-
Any other sickness insurance	1	2	2	3	2	2
Redundancy policy	2	2	1	2	1	2
Total households (base=100%)	**1,284**	**3,064**	**2,242**	**1,796**	**2,234**	**2,411**

Table 3.30: Continued

Percentage of households

				Government Office Region			
Insurance cover	London	South East	South West	England	Wales	Scotland	**Great Britain**
Mortgage protection	15	18	17	17	13	15	**16**
Personal accident	13	17	15	13	13	14	**13**
Private medical insurance	21	28	16	19	12	11	**17**
Permanent health insurance	5	5	4	4	2	3	**4**
Critical illness	6	6	5	5	3	4	**5**
Friendly society sickness insurance	2	2	2	2	1	-	**2**
Nursing home or long term care	1	1	-	-	-	-	**-**
Any other sickness insurance	2	2	2	2	2	2	**2**
Redundancy policy	1	1	1	1	1	2	**1**
Total households (base=100%)	**2,661**	**3,529**	**2,226**	**21,447**	**1,358**	**2,183**	**24,988**

Table 3.31: Households by insurance cover and age of head

Percentage of households

Insurance cover	Age: 16 to 24	25 to 34	35 to 44	45 to 54	55 to 59	60 to 64	65 to 74	75 to 84	85 or over	**Total households**
Mortgage protection	11	28	26	22	13	6	2	-	-	**16**
Personal accident	7	15	18	18	16	12	8	4	2	**13**
Private medical insurance	9	20	21	23	21	16	11	7	4	**17**
Permanent health insurance	1	6	5	5	4	2	1	1	0	**4**
Critical illness	3	11	9	5	3	1	-	-	0	**5**
Friendly society sickness insurance	0	2	2	3	3	3	2	2	1	**2**
Nursing home or long term care	-	1	-	-	-	-	-	-	0	**-**
Any other sickness insurance	-	2	3	2	2	2	1	1	-	**2**
Redundancy policy	1	3	2	2	1	-	-	0	0	**1**
Total households (base=100%)	**859**	**4,117**	**4,985**	**4,454**	**1,866**	**1,880**	**3,673**	**2,492**	**662**	**24,988**

DSS, Family Resources Survey Great Britain 1999-2000, © Crown Copyright 2001

Chapter 4

Tenure and housing costs

Introduction

Chapter 4 contains information on tenure and housing costs. The FRS primarily collects data on income, but housing costs is one area of household expenditure where detailed data are collected.

Total housing costs include all payments for water and sewerage charges, Council Tax Water Charge in Scotland, structural insurance and other charges on owner occupiers relating to their property (for example, ground rent and compulsory service charges). Figures for rent paid by respondents in rented accommodation are defined in terms of eligible rent, that is excluding charges which are not included in the calculation of Housing Benefit. For those buying their property with a mortgage, interest payments are included net of tax relief.

The Department uses the information on tenure and housing costs for the modelling and forecasting of benefits. They are also a key issue in the analysis of living standards. Housing costs vary across households. In part this reflects variations in the quality of housing, but there are also significant cost variations that do not reflect quality changes or differences. Further information on the use of housing costs in living standard analyses is given in the 1992 edition of Households Below Average Income analyses "HBAI 1979 to 1988/89" (TSO).

Contents and points to note when interpreting tables

Tables 4.1 to 4.5 provide information on tenure and type of accommodation. This information is split by household composition, age of head, ethnic group of head, length of residency of head and Government Office Region. The base used for these tables is all households. So, for example, Table 4.1 shows that 29 per cent of all households in the North East are rented from the Council. Accommodation type figures are split between rented and owner occupier households. Therefore, 11 per cent of all households are renters living in a purpose built flat or maisonette (Table 4.1). Overall, 15 per cent (11 per cent renters plus four per cent owner occupiers) of households live in this type of accommodation.

Table 4.5 considers length of residency of head for different tenure types and therefore provides information on mobility of households. However, as this question relates specifically to the head, it should be noted that other members of the household may have lived at the same address for shorter or longer periods.

Tables 4.6 to 4.10 provide information on weekly housing costs. Housing cost information is split by tenure and type of accommodation, age of head, ethnic group of head, household composition, Council Tax band and Government Office Region. Rent figures include any Housing Benefit in payment. Output categories are consistent with harmonisation, however, unlike harmonised inputs for mortgage interest, figures do not include any building insurance or other payments paid together with the mortgage repayment. More detailed information is given in the Glossary.

Table 4.11 looks at weekly rent amounts by region. Rent figures include any Housing Benefit in payment and the categories used are in line with harmonisation.

Key definitions used
(for a full explanation of all definitions please refer to the Glossary)

- Council Tax band
- Ethnic group
- Head of household
- Household rent

- Housing costs
- Sick or disabled adults
- Tenure

Changes to tables between 1998-1999 and 1999-2000

For consistency with other household composition tables in the publication, Tables 4.2 and 4.9 have been changed to show households without children before households with children.

Table 4.1: Households by tenure, type of accommodation and region

Tenure and type of accommodation	Government Office Region					
	North East	North West and Merseyside	Yorkshire and the Humber	East Midlands	West Midlands	Eastern
Rented accommodation						
Rented from:						
Council	29	15	22	16	18	13
Housing Association	3	6	4	4	6	4
All social rented sector tenants	32	20	26	19	24	17
Rented privately						
Unfurnished	6	5	5	6	5	6
Furnished	4	4	4	3	3	4
All rented privately	10	9	9	8	7	10
Accommodation						
House or bungalow						
Detached	2	1	1	2	1	2
Semi-detached	15	7	12	10	10	7
Terraced	14	12	12	8	10	9
All houses and bungalows	31	20	25	20	22	17
Flat or maisonette						
Purpose built	10	7	8	6	7	8
Non-purpose built	1	2	1	1	1	2
All flats or maisonettes	11	9	9	7	9	9
Other accommodation	-	-	1	-	-	-
Owner occupiers						
Tenure						
Owned outright	24	30	26	29	28	30
Buying with mortgage	34	41	39	43	41	43
All owners	58	71	65	72	69	73
Accommodation						
House or bungalow						
Detached	10	16	16	28	21	27
Semi-detached	24	29	27	29	28	24
Terraced	21	24	20	14	16	18
All houses and bungalows	55	69	63	72	65	69
Flat or maisonette						
Purpose built	2	1	1	1	3	3
Non-purpose built	1	1	1	-	-	1
All flats or maisonettes	3	2	2	1	4	4
Other accommodation	-	-	-	0	-	1
Total households (base=100%)	**1,284**	**3,064**	**2,242**	**1,796**	**2,234**	**2,411**

Percentage of households

Government Office Region

Tenure and type of accommodation	London	South East	South West	England	Wales	Scotland	**Great Britain**
Rented accommodation							
Rented from:							
Council	20	9	10	16	16	29	**17**
Housing Association	9	5	6	5	4	6	**5**
All social rented sector tenants	28	14	15	21	20	35	**22**
Rented privately							
Unfurnished	5	6	7	6	6	4	**5**
Furnished	9	5	5	5	5	4	**5**
All rented privately	14	11	12	10	11	8	**10**
Accommodation							
House or bungalow							
Detached	-	1	2	1	2	2	**1**
Semi-detached	2	5	6	8	7	6	**7**
Terraced	7	8	8	10	12	10	**10**
All houses and bungalows	10	14	17	18	22	18	**18**
Flat or maisonette							
Purpose built	25	8	6	10	5	24	**11**
Non-purpose built	6	2	4	3	3	1	**2**
All flats or maisonettes	31	10	10	13	8	25	**13**
Other accommodation	1	1	1	1	1	1	**1**
Owner occupiers							
Tenure							
Owned outright	20	29	33	28	36	20	**27**
Buying with mortgage	38	46	39	41	34	37	**40**
All owners	58	75	72	68	69	57	**67**
Accommodation							
House or bungalow							
Detached	5	28	27	20	22	15	**19**
Semi-detached	17	23	20	24	22	15	**23**
Terraced	22	18	19	19	24	14	**19**
All houses and bungalows	43	68	66	63	68	43	**62**
Flat or maisonette							
Purpose built	10	4	3	4	1	11	**4**
Non-purpose built	4	2	2	1	-	2	**1**
All flats or maisonettes	14	6	5	5	1	13	**5**
Other accommodation	-	1	1	-	-	-	**-**
Total households (base=100%)	**2,661**	**3,529**	**2,226**	**21,447**	**1,358**	**2,183**	**24,988**

DSS, Family Resources Survey Great Britain 1999-2000, © Crown Copyright 2001

Table 4.2: Households by tenure, type of accommodation and composition

Percentage of households

Tenure and type of accommodation	Households without children				Households with children			Total households
	One male adult	One female adult	Two adults	Three or more adults	One adult	Two adults	Three or more adults	
Rented accommodation								
Rented from:								
Council	23	25	10	12	42	12	16	**17**
Housing Association	8	9	3	2	15	4	4	**5**
All social rented sector tenants	31	34	13	14	56	16	20	**22**
Rented privately								
Unfurnished	7	7	5	3	9	5	3	**5**
Furnished	10	3	4	8	7	2	2	**5**
All rented privately	16	10	9	11	16	7	5	**10**
Accommodation								
House or bungalow								
Detached	1	1	1	1	1	2	1	**1**
Semi-detached	5	7	6	7	20	7	10	**7**
Terraced	8	11	6	11	30	9	10	**10**
All houses and bungalows	15	19	13	19	52	18	22	**18**
Flat or maisonette								
Purpose built	24	21	7	4	18	5	3	**11**
Non-purpose built	6	3	2	1	3	1	-	**2**
All flats or maisonettes	30	23	9	6	20	5	3	**13**
Other accommodation	3	1	-	-	-	-	0	**1**
Owner occupiers								
Tenure								
Owned outright	22	40	40	32	4	7	15	**27**
Buying with mortgage	31	16	37	43	23	70	60	**40**
All owners	53	56	77	75	27	77	75	**67**
Accommodation								
House or bungalow								
Detached	9	12	25	24	5	24	22	**19**
Semi-detached	14	17	27	29	9	29	29	**23**
Terraced	18	17	20	20	11	22	22	**19**
All houses and bungalows	41	46	72	73	25	74	74	**62**
Flat or maisonette								
Purpose built	8	8	4	1	1	2	1	**4**
Non-purpose built	3	2	1	-	1	1	-	**1**
All flats or maisonettes	11	10	5	2	2	2	1	**5**
Other accommodation	1	-	1	-	-	-	-	**-**
Total households (base=100%)	**2,982**	**4,269**	**8,079**	**1,656**	**1,834**	**5,325**	**843**	**24,988**

DSS, Family Resources Survey Great Britain 1999-2000, © Crown Copyright 2001

Table 4.2: Continued

Tenure and type of accommodation	Household composition		
	Households with one or more adults over pension age	Households with one or more sick or disabled adults under pension age	Households with one or more unemployed adults under pension age
Rented accommodation			
Rented from:			
Council	21	25	31
Housing Association	6	7	9
All social rented sector tenants	27	32	40
Rented privately			
Unfurnished	5	4	8
Furnished	1	5	9
All rented privately	6	9	17
Accommodation			
House or bungalow			
Detached	1	1	1
Semi-detached	8	10	12
Terraced	9	13	18
All houses and bungalows	18	24	31
Flat or maisonette			
Purpose built	13	14	20
Non-purpose built	1	3	5
All flats or maisonettes	14	17	25
Other accommodation	-	1	1
Owner occupiers			
Tenure			
Owned outright	57	21	13
Buying with mortgage	10	38	30
All owners	67	59	43
Accommodation			
House or bungalow			
Detached	21	15	11
Semi-detached	23	21	14
Terraced	16	19	15
All houses and bungalows	61	55	40
Flat or maisonette			
Purpose built	4	3	2
Non-purpose built	1	1	-
All flats or maisonettes	5	3	3
Other accommodation	1	-	-
Total households (base=100%)	8,225	5,228	1,309

DSS, Family Resources Survey Great Britain 1999-2000, © Crown Copyright 2001

Table 4.3: Households by tenure, type of accommodation and age of head

Tenure and type of accommodation	16 to 24	25 to 34	35 to 44	45 to 54	55 to 59	60 to 64	65 to 74	75 to 84	85 or over	Total households
Rented accommodation										
Rented from:										
Council	26	16	15	12	15	16	20	25	26	**17**
Housing Association	9	7	5	3	3	4	6	8	11	**5**
All social rented sector tenants	35	23	20	15	18	20	26	32	37	**22**
Rented privately										
Unfurnished	12	8	5	4	3	3	4	6	9	**5**
Furnished	32	11	4	2	1	1	1	1	2	**5**
All rented privately	44	20	9	6	4	5	4	7	11	**10**
Accommodation										
House or bungalow										
Detached	2	1	2	1	1	1	1	2	2	**1**
Semi-detached	11	9	7	5	6	5	8	10	9	**7**
Terraced	22	14	10	6	7	7	9	10	11	**10**
All houses and bungalows	36	24	19	13	13	14	17	21	23	**18**
Flat or maisonette										
Purpose built	28	13	8	7	7	9	12	17	23	**11**
Non-purpose built	11	5	2	1	1	1	1	1	1	**2**
All flats or maisonettes	39	18	10	8	8	10	13	17	24	**13**
Other accommodation	5	1	-	-	-	-	-	1	1	**1**
Owner occupiers										
Tenure										
Owned outright	2	2	6	19	37	52	62	58	50	**27**
Buying with mortgage	19	56	65	60	40	23	8	3	2	**40**
All owners	21	58	71	79	78	76	70	61	52	**67**
Accommodation										
House or bungalow										
Detached	-	7	19	27	28	27	22	19	15	**19**
Semi-detached	6	18	26	27	27	26	25	20	15	**23**
Terraced	10	23	21	21	19	18	17	14	12	**19**
All houses and bungalows	16	49	65	74	73	72	65	53	43	**62**
Flat or maisonette										
Purpose built	3	6	4	3	3	3	4	6	7	**4**
Non-purpose built	1	2	2	1	1	-	1	1	1	**1**
All flats or maisonettes	5	8	5	4	4	3	5	7	8	**5**
Other accommodation	0	-	-	-	1	1	1	-	1	**-**
Total households (base=100%)	**859**	**4,117**	**4,985**	**4,454**	**1,866**	**1,880**	**3,673**	**2,492**	**662**	**24,988**

DSS, Family Resources Survey Great Britain 1999-2000, © Crown Copyright 2001

Table 4.4: Households by tenure, type of accommodation and ethnic group of head

Percentage of households

Tenure and type of accommodation	White	Black	Indian	Pakistani/ Bangladeshi	Other	Total households
Rented accommodation						
Rented from:						
Council	17	30	8	25	18	**17**
Housing Association	5	19	4	8	9	**5**
All social rented sector tenants	22	49	13	33	26	**22**
Rented privately						
Unfurnished	5	5	3	3	5	**5**
Furnished	4	7	7	7	19	**5**
All rented privately	10	12	10	11	24	**10**
Accommodation						
House or bungalow						
Detached	1	-	0	1	1	**1**
Semi-detached	7	4	6	3	8	**7**
Terraced	10	12	9	14	9	**10**
All houses and bungalows	19	17	16	18	18	**18**
Flat or maisonette						
Purpose built	10	37	5	22	22	**11**
Non-purpose built	2	6	1	3	9	**3**
All flats or maisonettes	12	43	7	24	31	**13**
Other accommodation	1	1	-	2	2	**1**
Owner occupiers						
Tenure						
Owned outright	28	9	23	20	15	**27**
Buying with mortgage	40	29	54	36	35	**40**
All owners	68	39	77	56	50	**67**
Accommodation						
House or bungalow						
Detached	20	2	9	3	9	**19**
Semi-detached	24	9	31	16	17	**23**
Terraced	19	19	30	35	15	**19**
All houses and bungalows	63	31	70	54	41	**62**
Flat or maisonette						
Purpose built	4	5	4	2	8	**4**
Non-purpose built	1	3	3	1	1	**1**
All flats or maisonettes	5	8	7	2	9	**5**
Other accommodation	-	-	-	0	0	**-**
Total households (base=100%)	**23,760**	**438**	**236**	**248**	**306**	**24,988**

DSS, Family Resources Survey Great Britain 1999-2000, © Crown Copyright 2001

Table 4.5: Households by tenure, type of accommodation and length of residency of head

Percentage of households

Tenure and type of accommodation	Less than 12 months	12 months, less than 2 years	2 years, less than 3 years	3 years, less than 5 years	5 years, less than 10 years	10 years, less than 20 years	20 years or longer	Total households (base=100%)
Rented accommodation								
Rented from:								
Council	11	9	9	12	17	20	22	4,371
Housing Association	15	13	11	15	19	16	11	1,369
All social rented sector tenants	13	11	10	13	18	18	16	5,740
Rented privately								
Unfurnished	29	15	10	8	9	11	18	1,387
Furnished	50	22	9	9	5	3	2	1,021
All rented privately	40	18	9	8	7	7	10	2,408
Accommodation								
House or bungalow								
Detached	21	12	9	10	15	16	18	370
Semi-detached	15	11	9	9	15	17	25	1,936
Terraced	19	12	9	12	13	17	19	2,510
All houses and bungalows	18	11	9	10	14	16	20	4,816
Flat or maisonette								
Purpose built	19	13	11	13	16	16	12	2,659
Non-purpose built	39	18	8	10	11	8	4	529
All flats or maisonettes	29	16	9	11	14	12	8	3,188
Other accommodation	36	21	11	9	7	9	6	144
Owner occupiers								
Tenure								
Owned outright	3	3	3	4	9	22	55	6,978
Buying with mortgage	9	10	9	12	21	28	12	9,862
All owners	6	6	6	8	15	25	33	16,840
Accommodation								
House or bungalow								
Detached	6	6	7	9	17	29	25	5,080
Semi-detached	6	6	6	8	14	25	36	5,862
Terraced	7	8	7	9	16	24	31	4,540
All houses and bungalows	6	7	6	9	16	26	30	15,482
Flat or maisonette								
Purpose built	11	12	9	11	22	21	14	952
Non-purpose built	17	13	8	12	21	19	9	313
All flats or maisonettes	14	12	9	11	22	20	12	1,265
Other accommodation	10	8	2	8	27	25	19	93
Total households	11	9	8	10	16	22	25	24,988

DSS, Family Resources Survey Great Britain 1999-2000, © Crown Copyright 2001

Table 4.6: Households by tenure, type of accommodation and weekly housing costs

Percentage of households

Tenure and type of accommodation	Under £20 a week	£20 but under £40 a week	£40 but under £60 a week	£60 but under £80 a week	£80 but under £100 a week	£100 but under £150 a week	£150 a week or more	Total households (base = 100%)
Rented accommodation								
Rented from:								
Council	1	29	57	11	2	-	-	4,371
Housing Association	1	10	46	30	8	3	2	1,369
All social rented sector tenants	1	20	51	21	5	2	1	5,740
Rented privately								
Unfurnished	24	9	15	20	14	12	6	1,387
Furnished	8	6	12	19	15	20	19	1,021
All rented privately	16	8	14	20	15	16	12	2,408
Accommodation								
House or bungalow								
Detached	35	10	13	14	8	11	9	370
Semi-detached	7	19	49	13	4	5	3	1,936
Terraced	4	17	44	18	8	5	4	2,510
All houses and bungalows	16	16	35	15	7	7	5	4,816
Flat or maisonette								
Purpose built	3	24	43	18	5	4	3	2,659
Non-purpose built	3	7	24	28	15	12	11	529
All flats or maisonettes	3	16	33	23	10	8	7	3,188
Other accommodation	13	28	34	10	5	6	4	144
Owner occupiers								
Tenure								
Owned outright	96	3	-	-	-	0	-	6,978
Buying with mortgage	9	23	26	19	11	9	4	9,862
All owners	53	13	13	9	5	5	2	16,840
Accommodation								
House or bungalow								
Detached	49	10	11	9	8	9	5	5,080
Semi-detached	46	14	16	12	6	4	2	5,862
Terraced	42	19	18	11	5	3	1	4,540
All houses and bungalows	46	14	15	11	6	6	2	15,482
Flat or maisonette								
Purpose built	35	21	20	12	7	5	1	952
Non-purpose built	29	15	18	15	8	8	7	313
All flats or maisonettes	32	18	19	14	7	6	4	1,265
Other accommodation	30	56	3	6	1	3	0	93
Total households	**32**	**16**	**24**	**13**	**6**	**6**	**3**	**24,988**

DSS, Family Resources Survey Great Britain 1999-2000, © Crown Copyright 2001

Table 4.7: Households by age of head and weekly housing costs

	Housing costs			
Age	Under £20 a week	£20 but under £40 a week	£40 but under £60 a week	£60 but under £80 a week
16 to 24	5	16	33	18
25 to 34	4	13	32	23
35 to 44	10	16	29	20
45 to 54	27	21	23	12
55 to 59	44	20	19	9
60 to 64	59	15	17	5
65 to 74	65	13	16	4
75 to 84	60	15	18	5
85 or over	54	15	22	6
Total households	**32**	**16**	**24**	**13**

Table 4.7: Continued

Percentage of households

	Housing costs			
Age	£80 but under £100 a week	£100 but under £150 a week	£150 a week or more	Total households (base = 100%)
16 to 24	9	10	8	859
25 to 34	13	10	5	4,117
35 to 44	10	10	5	4,985
45 to 54	7	6	3	4,454
55 to 59	3	3	1	1,866
60 to 64	2	1	-	1,880
65 to 74	1	-	-	3,673
75 to 84	1	1	-	2,492
85 or over	2	1	1	662
Total households	**6**	**6**	**3**	**24,988**

Table 4.8: Households by ethnic group of head and weekly housing costs

Percentage of households

Ethnic group	Housing costs			
	Under £20 a week	£20 but under £40 a week	£40 but under £60 a week	£60 but under £80 a week
White	33	17	24	13
Black	13	9	33	20
Indian	32	12	22	13
Pakistani/Bangladeshi	28	16	25	18
Other	18	5	21	17
Total households	**32**	**16**	**24**	**13**

Table 4.8: Continued

Percentage of households

Ethnic group	Housing costs			Total households (base = 100%)
	£80 but under £100 a week	£100 but under £150 a week	£150 a week or more	
White	6	5	3	**23,760**
Black	13	9	4	**438**
Indian	11	7	4	**236**
Pakistani/Bangladeshi	4	4	4	**248**
Other	13	12	13	**306**
Total households	**6**	**6**	**3**	**24,988**

DSS, Family Resources Survey Great Britain 1999-2000, © Crown Copyright 2001

Table 4.9: Households by composition and weekly housing costs

Percentage of households

Household composition	Housing costs			
	Under £20 a week	£20 but under £40 a week	£40 but under £60 a week	£60 but under £80 a week
Households without children				
One adult				
adult male	25	21	29	15
adult female	44	17	24	10
Two adults	45	14	18	10
Three or more adults	39	19	18	8
Households with children				
One adult	7	15	40	22
Two adults	11	15	27	20
Three or more adults	21	19	26	16
Total households without children	**40**	**17**	**22**	**10**
Total households with children	**12**	**16**	**29**	**20**
Households with one or more adults over pension age	*61*	*14*	*17*	*5*
Households with one or more sick or disabled adults under pension age	*27*	*19*	*28*	*13*
Households with one or more unemployed adults under pension age	*17*	*19*	*33*	*15*

Table 4.9: Continued

Household composition	Housing costs			Total
	£80 but under £100 a week	£100 but under £150 a week	£150 a week or more	Total households (base = 100%)
Households without children				
One adult				
adult male	5	4	2	**2,982**
adult female	3	2	1	**4,269**
Two adults	6	5	2	**8,079**
Three or more adults	3	6	6	**1,656**
Households with children				
One adult	10	5	2	**1,834**
Two adults	11	11	6	**5,325**
Three or more adults	8	6	4	**843**
Total households without children	**5**	**4**	**2**	**16,986**
Total households with children	**11**	**9**	**5**	**8,002**
Households with one or more adults over pension age	*1*	*1*	-	*8,225*
Households with one or more sick or disabled adults under pension age	*6*	*4*	*2*	*5,228*
Households with one or more unemployed adults under pension age	*7*	*5*	*4*	*1,309*

Table 4.10: Households by Council Tax band and weekly housing costs

	Housing costs			
Council Tax band	Under £20 a week	£20 but under £40 a week	£40 but under £60 a week	£60 but under £80 a week
Band A	21	28	38	9
Band B	29	17	32	16
Band C	35	12	19	19
Band D	39	10	13	15
Band E	42	8	10	9
Band F	45	10	9	7
Band G	43	8	6	7
Band H	29	23	11	4
Not valued separately	29	19	18	11
Total households	**32**	**16**	**24**	**13**

Table 4.10: Continued

Percentage of households

	Housing costs			
Council Tax band	£80 but under £100 a week	£100 but under £150 a week	£150 a week or more	Total households (base = 100%)
Band A	3	1	-	6,204
Band B	5	2	-	4,859
Band C	8	6	2	5,112
Band D	11	9	4	4,064
Band E	10	14	7	2,288
Band F	6	12	12	1,185
Band G	6	13	16	847
Band H	4	9	20	132
Not valued separately	5	11	6	297
Total households	**6**	**6**	**3**	**24,988**

Table 4.11: Households in rented accommodation by region and weekly rent

Percentage of households

Government Office Region	Under £20 a week	£20 but under £40 a week	£40 but under £60 a week	£60 but under £80 a week
North East	6	47	35	7
North West and Merseyside	5	25	47	13
Yorkshire and the Humber	6	52	26	9
East Midlands	8	35	41	10
West Midlands	5	31	45	8
Eastern	6	15	46	16
London	4	4	36	24
South East	9	10	36	21
South West	9	17	38	21
England	6	24	39	16
Wales	8	32	42	9
Scotland	7	58	25	4
Great Britain	**6**	**28**	**37**	**14**

Table 4.11: Continued

Percentage of households

Government Office Region	£80 but under £100 a week	£100 but under £150 a week	£150 a week or more	Total households (base = 100%)
North East	3	1	-	547
North West and Merseyside	6	3	1	904
Yorkshire and the Humber	3	2	1	794
East Midlands	3	2	1	499
West Midlands	5	4	1	697
Eastern	8	6	3	661
London	7	11	14	1,163
South East	9	10	6	898
South West	7	5	2	614
England	6	6	4	6,777
Wales	4	3	2	423
Scotland	3	3	1	948
Great Britain	**5**	**5**	**4**	**8,148**

DSS, Family Resources Survey Great Britain 1999-2000, © Crown Copyright 2001

Chapter 5

Assets and savings

Introduction

All adults questioned in the FRS are asked about their types of accounts, investments and interest received over the last 12 months.

For benefit units who estimate the value of all their investments to be in the range of £1,500 to £20,000, further questions are asked in respect of the actual value of their holdings. For benefit units whose total savings fall outside this range, the value of their total investments are estimated based on the interest they earn from individual accounts. Only around two fifths of all respondents are asked the detailed questions on their assets and savings.

Data are not available for amounts held in individual accounts or average amounts of savings because this information is not collected for all respondents.

Contents and points to note when interpreting tables

The data relating to assets and savings should be treated with caution. Questions relating to assets are a sensitive section of the questionnaire and have the lowest response rate. A high proportion of respondents do not know the interest received on their assets and therefore around one in ten cases are imputed (Chapter 8 outlines the imputation methods undertaken). Evidence also suggests that there is some under reporting of capital by respondents, in terms of both the actual value of the assets and the investment income (see Chapter 3 for further details). A comparison of FRS and the Family Expenditure Survey (FES) data for pensioners supported this and illustrated that the proportion of pensioners holding stocks and shares was lower on the FRS compared to the FES. This suggests that the FRS may also under account the level of assets that yield an income stream.

Tables 5.1 to 5.8 illustrate the type of accounts and savings that were held by households, benefit units and individuals. The amounts of savings held are displayed in Tables 5.9 to 5.11 on a household and benefit unit level. Tables of total capital holdings are given in the bands that reflect the original estimate made by respondents and capital limits for different types of benefit and support.

Table 5.12 shows households by amount of savings and gross weekly household income. This shows broadly what would be expected: households with larger income have more capital. Any deviations from this pattern may be due to reporting problems with income and capital already highlighted. Individual figures in this table should be treated with caution.

Key definitions used
(for a full explanation of all definitions please refer to the Glossary)

- Any type of account
- Economic status
- Ethnic group
- Family status

- Gross weekly household income
- Head of benefit unit
- Head of household

Changes to tables between 1998-1999 and 1999-2000

The tables now cover accounts held by adults only as questions for children's accounts are no longer asked.

Data on Individual Savings Accounts (ISA) were collected in the survey from 1999/2000 and are included in tables 5.1 to 5.8.

This year data are also included for accounts capable of accepting Automated Credit Transfers (ACT). The accounts covered by this are Current, Post Office and other bank/building society.

There has been a concern for some time that the FRS on average has picked up fewer savings accounts and investments than the FES and some other surveys. There could be a number of reasons for this, but one theory is that the method of questioning is having an effect. To check for this, we have added a Yes/No question at the start of the 'accounts' section to pick up any type of account.

For consistency with other household composition tables in the publication, Tables 5.2 and 5.9 have been changed to show households without children before households with children.

DSS, Family Resources Survey Great Britain 1999-2000, © Crown Copyright 2001

Table 5.1: Households by type of saving and region

		Government Office Region				
Type of account	North East	North West and Merseyside	Yorkshire and the Humber	East Midlands	West Midlands	Eastern
Current account	76	85	85	86	83	90
Post Office account	4	8	8	8	6	10
TESSA	10	15	13	16	14	17
ISA	8	11	10	11	10	11
Other bank/building society accounts	47	56	59	65	65	69
Gilts	1	1	1	-	1	1
Unit trusts	3	5	4	5	5	6
Stocks and shares	17	26	24	25	23	31
National Savings Bonds	2	5	4	5	5	6
Save As You Earn	1	2	2	2	1	2
Premium Bonds	16	24	23	27	23	33
PEPs	8	13	11	13	13	15
Any type of account	84	90	92	93	92	96
No accounts	16	10	8	7	8	4
ACT Compatible Account	83	89	92	93	91	95
Total households (base=100%)	**1,284**	**3,064**	**2,242**	**1,796**	**2,234**	**2,411**

Table 5.1: Continued

		Government Office Region					**Great**
Type of account	London	South East	South West	England	Wales	Scotland	**Britain**
Current account	84	91	91	86	84	78	**86**
Post Office account	7	11	11	8	7	5	**8**
TESSA	13	18	17	15	13	11	**14**
ISA	10	13	14	11	10	9	**11**
Other bank/building society accounts	57	72	65	62	53	53	**61**
Gilts	1	2	1	1	1	1	**1**
Unit trusts	6	8	8	6	4	5	**6**
Stocks and shares	27	36	29	27	19	22	**26**
National Savings Bonds	4	7	8	5	5	4	**5**
Save As You Earn	2	2	2	2	1	1	**2**
Premium Bonds	25	36	33	27	21	16	**26**
PEPs	14	19	16	14	12	11	**14**
Any type of account	90	96	96	92	89	87	**92**
No accounts	10	4	4	8	11	13	**8**
ACT Compatible Account	90	96	95	92	89	87	**91**
Total households (base=100%)	**2,661**	**3,529**	**2,226**	**21,447**	**1,358**	**2,183**	**24,988**

DSS, Family Resources Survey Great Britain 1999-2000, © Crown Copyright 2001

Table 5.2: Households by type of saving and composition

Percentage of households

Type of account	Households without children				Households with children			Total households
	One male adult	One female adult	Two adults	Three or more adults	One adult	Two adults	Three or more adults	
Current account	78	75	91	95	59	92	93	86
Post Office account	5	9	9	13	3	6	11	8
TESSA	9	13	20	19	2	12	10	14
ISA	8	9	15	16	2	9	9	11
Other bank/building society accounts	49	55	69	73	30	64	65	61
Gilts	1	1	1	1	-	1	-	1
Unit trusts	5	5	8	7	1	4	4	6
Stocks and shares	20	18	33	34	6	29	27	26
National Savings Bonds	4	7	8	6	-	2	3	5
Save As You Earn	1	1	2	2	1	3	2	2
Premium Bonds	17	20	34	35	7	25	27	26
PEPs	10	10	19	18	2	12	11	14
Any type of account	86	88	96	97	71	95	96	92
No accounts	14	12	4	3	29	5	4	8
ACT Compatible Account	86	87	95	97	70	95	96	91
Total households (base=100%)	2,982	4,269	8,079	1,656	1,834	5,325	843	24,988

Table 5.2: Continued

Percentage of households

Type of account	Household composition		
	Households with one or more adults over pension age	Households with one or more sick or disabled adults under pension age	Households with one or more unemployed adults under pension age
Current account	80	79	72
Post Office account	9	7	6
TESSA	18	10	6
ISA	12	9	5
Other bank/building society accounts	61	51	42
Gilts	2	-	-
Unit trusts	7	3	3
Stocks and shares	26	20	14
National Savings Bonds	11	3	2
Save As You Earn	1	1	1
Premium Bonds	30	23	16
PEPs	15	10	6
Any type of account	91	85	80
No accounts	9	15	20
ACT Compatible Account	91	85	80
Total households (base=100%)	8,225	5,228	1,309

DSS, Family Resources Survey Great Britain 1999-2000, © Crown Copyright 2001

Table 5.3: Households by type of saving and age of head

				Percentage of households
		Age		

Type of account	16 to 24	25 to 34	35 to 44	45 to 54	55 to 59
Current account	77	86	89	91	89
Post Office account	10	7	6	8	9
TESSA	4	7	10	18	21
ISA	4	9	9	13	16
Other bank/building society accounts	42	56	61	67	65
Gilts	-	-	-	1	1
Unit trusts	2	3	4	6	8
Stocks and shares	11	20	26	33	34
National Savings Bonds	3	1	1	3	4
Save As You Earn	-	2	2	2	1
Premium Bonds	10	15	23	32	35
PEPs	3	8	11	17	23
Any type of account	83	90	93	94	93
No accounts	17	10	7	6	7
ACT Compatible Account	82	90	93	94	92
Total households (base=100%)	**859**	**4,117**	**4,985**	**4,454**	**1,866**

Table 5.3: Continued

				Percentage of households
		Age		

Type of account	60 to 64	65 to 74	75 to 84	85 or over	Total households
Current account	87	82	76	69	**86**
Post Office account	7	9	10	13	**8**
TESSA	26	20	14	8	**14**
ISA	15	13	9	6	**11**
Other bank/building society accounts	63	62	62	53	**61**
Gilts	2	2	2	2	**1**
Unit trusts	10	8	6	4	**6**
Stocks and shares	32	29	22	17	**26**
National Savings Bonds	8	11	12	9	**5**
Save As You Earn	2	1	-	-	**2**
Premium Bonds	36	31	28	21	**26**
PEPs	23	17	10	4	**14**
Any type of account	93	92	91	87	**92**
No accounts	7	8	9	13	**8**
ACT Compatible Account	93	91	90	86	**91**
Total households (base=100%)	**1,880**	**3,673**	**2,492**	**662**	**24,988**

Table 5.4: Households by type of saving and ethnic group of head

Percentage of households

| Type of account | Ethnic group | | | | | Total households |
	White	Black	Indian	Pakistani/ Bangladeshi	Other	
Current account	86	73	88	74	85	86
Post Office account	8	5	7	4	2	8
TESSA	15	5	16	2	7	14
ISA	11	7	7	2	6	11
Other bank/building society accounts	62	40	54	34	43	61
Gilts	1	0	0	0	-	1
Unit trusts	6	1	5	0	2	6
Stocks and shares	27	14	25	8	18	26
National Savings Bonds	5	-	1	-	1	5
Save As You Earn	2	1	2	1	1	2
Premium Bonds	27	9	14	5	11	26
PEPs	14	5	14	3	7	14
Any type of account	92	83	93	83	89	92
No accounts	8	17	7	17	11	8
ACT Compatible Account	92	83	93	83	89	91
Total households (base=100%)	**23,760**	**438**	**236**	**248**	**306**	**24,998**

DSS, Family Resources Survey Great Britain 1999-2000, © Crown Copyright 2001

Table 5.5: Benefit units by type of saving and family status

Percentage of benefit units

Type of account	Pensioner couple	Single male pensioner	Single female pensioner	Couple with children	Couple without children	Single with children	Single male without children	Single female without children	Total benefit units
				Family status					
Current account	86	73	68	92	93	61	78	83	**83**
Post Office account	11	5	9	6	7	3	5	7	**7**
TESSA	21	12	12	11	20	2	5	7	**12**
ISA	14	9	8	9	15	2	6	7	**9**
Other bank/building society accounts	66	54	54	64	69	29	40	46	**55**
Gilts	2	2	1	-	1	-	-	-	**1**
Unit trusts	9	6	5	4	7	1	3	2	**5**
Stocks and shares	31	21	17	29	34	6	13	11	**22**
National Savings Bonds	14	8	8	2	4	-	2	2	**4**
Save As You Earn	1	-	-	3	3	1	1	1	**1**
Premium Bonds	37	21	20	25	34	8	12	12	**22**
PEPs	19	10	8	12	20	2	6	6	**11**
Any type of account	95	87	85	95	96	72	85	88	**90**
No accounts	5	13	15	5	4	28	15	12	**10**
ACT Compatible Account	94	87	85	95	96	71	85	88	**89**
Total benefit units (base=100%)	**2,966**	**1,186**	**3,452**	**5,862**	**5,757**	**2,131**	**4,786**	**3,435**	**29,575**

Table 5.6: Benefit units by type of saving and economic status

Percentage of benefit units

| Type of account | | Economic status | | | |
	Self employed	Single or couple, all in full time work	Couple, one in full time work, one in part time work	Couple, one in full time work, one not working	One or more in part time work
Current account	95	93	97	94	86
Post Office account	7	6	7	6	7
TESSA	15	10	17	14	14
ISA	11	10	13	12	10
Other bank/building society accounts	65	59	72	64	51
Gilts	1	-	-	1	1
Unit trusts	5	3	5	7	6
Stocks and shares	32	23	35	30	21
National Savings Bonds	3	2	3	3	4
Save As You Earn	1	2	3	2	1
Premium Bonds	30	19	32	29	22
PEPs	16	10	15	17	13
Any type of account	98	97	99	97	93
No accounts	2	3	1	3	7
ACT Compatible Account	97	97	99	97	93
Total benefit units (base=100%)	**2,009**	**7,998**	**2,761**	**2,264**	**2,400**

Table 5.6: Continued

Percentage of benefit units

| Type of account | | Economic status | | | Total benefit units |
	Head or spouse aged 60 or over	Head or spouse unemployed	Head or spouse sick or disabled	Others	
Current account	75	53	49	63	83
Post Office account	9	4	4	6	7
TESSA	16	2	3	5	12
ISA	10	1	2	3	9
Other bank/building society accounts	57	24	24	30	55
Gilts	2	-	-	-	1
Unit trusts	6	1	1	2	5
Stocks and shares	22	4	6	8	22
National Savings Bonds	10	1	1	1	4
Save As You Earn	-	0	-	-	1
Premium Bonds	26	7	8	9	22
PEPs	13	1	3	5	11
Any type of account	89	64	61	71	90
No accounts	11	36	39	29	10
ACT Compatible Account	88	64	60	71	89
Total benefit units (base=100%)	**7,691**	**1,149**	**1,760**	**1,543**	**29,575**

DSS, Family Resources Survey Great Britain 1999-2000, © Crown Copyright 2001

Table 5.7: Adults by sex, type of saving and age

Percentage of adults

	Age				
Type of account	16 to 24	25 to 34	35 to 44	45 to 54	55 to 59
Male					
Current account	77	86	87	89	86
Post Office account	6	4	3	4	4
TESSA	2	5	8	14	18
ISA	3	7	8	9	11
Other bank/building society accounts	32	49	53	56	55
Gilts	-	0	-	1	1
Unit trusts	1	2	4	5	7
Stocks and shares	6	17	23	28	30
National Savings Bonds	1	1	1	2	3
Save As You Earn	-	2	1	2	1
Premium Bonds	7	11	16	25	27
PEPs	1	7	10	15	20
Any type of account	85	91	92	93	91
No accounts	15	9	8	7	9
ACT Compatible Account	85	90	91	93	90
Total males (base=100%)	**1,944**	**3,747**	**4,136**	**3,747**	**1,536**
Female					
Current account	79	83	85	87	85
Post Office account	7	5	4	6	6
TESSA	2	6	8	17	20
ISA	3	6	6	10	12
Other bank/building society accounts	36	53	56	60	59
Gilts	-	-	-	1	1
Unit trusts	-	2	2	5	7
Stocks and shares	4	13	18	24	24
National Savings Bonds	1	1	1	3	5
Save As You Earn	-	2	1	1	1
Premium Bonds	6	10	16	26	24
PEPs	1	6	8	14	18
Any type of account	85	89	91	92	92
No accounts	15	11	9	8	8
ACT Compatible Account	84	89	90	91	91
Total females (base=100%)	**2,138**	**4,225**	**4,521**	**3,931**	**1,634**

Table 5.7: Continued

Type of account	Age 16 to 24	25 to 34	35 to 44	45 to 54	55 to 59
Total adults					
Current account	78	85	86	88	85
Post Office account	6	5	4	5	5
TESSA	2	5	8	15	19
ISA	3	7	7	10	12
Other bank/building society accounts	34	51	54	58	57
Gilts	-	-	-	1	1
Unit trusts	1	2	3	5	7
Stocks and shares	5	15	21	26	27
National Savings Bonds	1	1	1	2	4
Save As You Earn	-	2	1	2	1
Premium Bonds	6	11	16	25	26
PEPs	1	6	9	14	19
Any type of account	85	90	91	92	91
No accounts	15	10	9	8	9
ACT Compatible Account	85	89	91	92	90
Total adults (base =100%)	**4,092**	**7,972**	**8,657**	**7,678**	**3,170**

DSS, Family Resources Survey Great Britain 1999-2000, © Crown Copyright 2001

Table 5.7: Continued

Type of account	Age 60 to 64	65 to 74	75 to 84	85 or over	Total adults
Male					
Current account	85	82	79	72	85
Post Office account	4	5	7	10	4
TESSA	22	18	12	10	11
ISA	11	12	9	7	8
Other bank/building society accounts	54	56	59	55	51
Gilts	1	1	2	3	1
Unit trusts	10	8	6	6	4
Stocks and shares	29	27	21	20	22
National Savings Bonds	5	8	11	9	3
Save As You Earn	1	-	-	0	1
Premium Bonds	29	27	26	20	19
PEPs	22	18	10	5	11
Any type of account	91	92	92	89	91
No accounts	9	8	8	11	9
ACT Compatible Account	91	91	91	89	90
Total males **(base=100%)**	1,477	2,526	1,341	275	20,729
Female					
Current account	83	76	68	61	81
Post Office account	6	9	9	14	6
TESSA	22	16	12	4	12
ISA	12	11	7	3	8
Other bank/building society accounts	58	59	58	48	55
Gilts	2	2	2	1	1
Unit trusts	7	6	4	2	4
Stocks and shares	25	21	16	11	18
National Savings Bonds	8	10	10	10	4
Save As You Earn	1	-	-	0	1
Premium Bonds	26	25	22	16	18
PEPs	19	13	7	3	10
Any type of account	90	89	87	83	89
No accounts	10	11	13	17	11
ACT Compatible Account	90	88	86	82	89
Total females **(base=100%)**	1,669	2,814	1,926	520	23,378

Percentage of adults

Type of account	Age				Total adults
	60 to 64	65 to 74	75 to 84	85 or over	
Total adults					
Current account	84	79	72	65	83
Post Office account	5	7	8	13	5
TESSA	22	17	12	6	11
ISA	12	11	8	4	8
Other bank/building society accounts	56	58	58	50	53
Gilts	1	2	2	1	1
Unit trusts	8	7	5	3	4
Stocks and shares	27	24	18	14	20
National Savings Bonds	7	9	11	9	3
Save As You Earn	1	-	-	0	1
Premium Bonds	27	26	24	17	19
PEPs	20	15	8	3	11
Any type of account	91	90	89	85	90
No accounts	9	10	11	15	10
ACT Compatible Account	90	90	88	84	90
Total adults **(base =100%)**	3,146	5,340	3,267	795	44,107

DSS, Family Resources Survey Great Britain 1999-2000, © Crown Copyright 2001

Table 5.8: Households by type of saving and gross weekly household income

Percentage of households

Type of account	Under £100 a week	£100 and less than £200	£200 and less than £300	£300 and less than £400	£400 and less than £500	£500 and less than £600	£600 and less than £700	£700 and above	Total households
Current account	68	66	79	92	96	98	98	99	86
Post Office account	9	6	7	8	8	9	8	10	8
TESSA	6	6	10	14	17	17	18	26	14
ISA	4	5	8	11	12	13	14	21	11
Other bank/building society accounts	45	42	48	59	68	74	77	85	61
Gilts	1	-	1	1	1	1	1	2	1
Unit trusts	2	2	3	5	6	7	7	11	6
Stocks and shares	13	10	18	24	29	33	37	49	26
National Savings Bonds	5	5	5	5	5	4	4	6	5
Save As You Earn	-	-	1	1	2	2	3	4	2
Premium Bonds	16	16	21	26	27	31	33	41	26
PEPs	5	4	8	13	15	17	18	28	14
Any type of account	82	79	88	96	99	99	99	100	92
No accounts	18	21	12	4	1	1	1	-	8
ACT Compatible Account	82	79	88	96	98	99	98	100	91
Total households (base=100%)	1,345	5,721	4,247	2,950	2,475	2,123	1,604	4,523	24,988

DSS, Family Resources Survey Great Britain 1999-2000, © Crown Copyright 2001

Table 5.9: Households by amount of savings and composition

Capital	Households without children				Households with children			Total households
	One male adult	One female adult	Two adults	Three or more adults	One adult	Two adults	Three or more adults	
No savings	35	29	18	16	68	28	25	27
Less than £1,500	23	24	19	22	23	29	29	23
£1,500 but less than £3,000	8	9	8	8	3	9	8	8
£3,000 but less than £8,000	13	14	15	17	4	15	14	14
£8,000 but less than £10,000	3	3	4	5	-	3	3	3
£10,000 but less than £16,000	5	6	8	9	1	5	8	7
£16,000 but less than £20,000	2	2	4	4	-	2	3	3
£20,000 or more	12	13	23	19	1	10	9	15
Total households (base=100%)	**2,982**	**4,269**	**8,079**	**1,656**	**1,834**	**5,325**	**843**	**24,988**

Table 5.9: Continued

Capital	Household composition		
	Households with one or more adults over pension age	*Households with one or more sick or disabled adults under pension age*	*Households with one or more unemployed adults under pension age*
No savings	21	39	53
Less than £1,500	18	25	22
£1,500 but less than £3,000	8	6	5
£3,000 but less than £8,000	14	11	8
£8,000 but less than £10,000	3	2	2
£10,000 but less than £16,000	8	5	2
£16,000 but less than £20,000	3	2	1
£20,000 or more	24	10	7
Total households (base=100%)	**8,225**	**5,228**	**1,309**

Table 5.10: Benefit units by amount of savings and family status

Capital	Pensioner couple	Single male pensioner	Single female pensioner	Couple with children	Couple without children	Single with children	Single male without children	Single female without children	**Total benefit units**
No savings	16	26	29	27	19	67	47	45	**33**
Less than £1,500	15	19	21	30	21	23	26	30	**24**
£1,500 but less than £3,000	7	9	10	8	8	3	7	7	**8**
£3,000 but less than £8,000	13	14	14	15	16	4	10	10	**13**
£8,000 but less than £10,000	4	3	3	3	4	1	2	1	**3**
£10,000 but less than £16,000	9	6	6	6	8	1	3	3	**5**
£16,000 but less than £20,000	4	3	3	2	4	-	1	1	**2**
£20,000 or more	32	20	14	9	19	1	5	3	**12**
Total benefit units (base=100%)	**2,966**	**1,186**	**3,452**	**5,862**	**5,757**	**2,131**	**4,786**	**3,435**	**29,575**

Table 5.11: Benefit units by amount of savings and economic status

Capital	Self employed	Single or couple, all in full time work	Couple, one in full time work, one in part time work	Couple, one in full time work, one not working	One or more in part time work
No savings	20	29	17	25	38
Less than £1,500	25	30	28	26	24
£1,500 but less than £3,000	9	9	10	8	6
£3,000 but less than £8,000	17	14	17	14	10
£8,000 but less than £10,000	3	3	4	4	2
£10,000 but less than £16,000	7	5	7	7	5
£16,000 but less than £20,000	4	2	3	3	2
£20,000 or more	15	7	14	15	14
Total benefit units (base=100%)	**2,009**	**7,998**	**2,761**	**2,264**	**2,400**

Table 5.11: Continued

Percentage of benefit units

Capital	Head or spouse aged 60 or over	Head or spouse unemployed	Head or spouse sick or disabled	Others	Total benefit units
No savings	25	74	70	64	**33**
Less than £1,500	18	17	18	19	**24**
£1,500 but less than £3,000	8	3	3	3	**8**
£3,000 but less than £8,000	13	3	3	6	**13**
£8,000 but less than £10,000	3	-	1	-	**3**
£10,000 but less than £16,000	7	1	1	1	**5**
£16,000 but less than £20,000	3	-	-	1	**2**
£20,000 or more	22	2	4	7	**12**
Total benefit units (base=100%)	**7,691**	**1,149**	**1,760**	**1,543**	**29,575**

DSS, Family Resources Survey Great Britain 1999-2000, © Crown Copyright 2001

Table 5.12: Households by amount of savings and gross weekly household income

Capital	Under £100 a week	£100 and less than £200	£200 and less than £300	£300 and less than £400	£400 and less than £500	£500 and less than £600	£600 and less than £700	£700 and above	Total households
Gross weekly household income									
No savings	40	45	38	27	20	16	12	7	27
Less than £1,500	22	23	22	27	28	27	28	18	23
£1,500 but less than £3,000	9	7	7	7	8	10	10	8	8
£3,000 but less than £8,000	14	10	11	13	15	16	18	19	14
£8,000 but less than £10,000	2	2	2	3	3	4	4	5	3
£10,000 but less than £16,000	4	4	6	6	6	8	8	10	7
£16,000 but less than £20,000	2	2	2	2	2	3	4	5	3
£20,000 or more	7	7	13	16	17	16	16	28	15
Total households (base=100%)	1,345	5,721	4,247	2,950	2,475	2,123	1,604	4,523	24,988

Chapter 6

Carers

Introduction

The FRS collects information on those giving and receiving help on an informal basis, that is, not as part of a paid job. What should be counted as care is not prescriptively defined. Respondents are asked if anyone in the household provides care to anyone living outside the household. Questions then ask who is receiving the help or being looked after and then there are follow-up questions for each person named, who

provides the help and how frequently they receive the help. Note that the follow-up questions are only asked for those receiving help at least once a week.

Information on carers and those receiving care is used within the DSS in the modelling of benefits, such as Invalid Care Allowance and Disability Living Allowance, as well as in analyses of work incentive issues.

Contents and points to note when interpreting tables

Tables 6.1 to 6.4 look at those providing care. Carers are counted only once, even if they look after more than one individual. Carers outside the household are not included in these tables as they are not identified individually within the questionnaire, and they may also produce instances of double counting. Information is now collected for individual children who are carers in the same way that it is for adults. Therefore these tables, with the exception of Table 6.3, which looks at employment status, show statistics for *all* informal carers.

Table 6.2 gives the relationship between the carer and the person being cared for. Those giving care to more than one person have been combined into one group. For non-household members, more than one person receiving care means more than one entry in either the "relative", "friend or neighbour", "client of voluntary organisation" or "other non-household" group. However, if, for example, someone cared for more than one friend or neighbour, this would not be picked up by the questionnaire.

Table 6.3 shows the employment status of adult carers, using ILO definitions of employment in harmonisation with other government surveys.

Tables 6.5 and 6.6 look at household members receiving care. An individual is recorded as receiving care if they receive care from another person in the household, and/or from someone outside the household. They are counted only once no matter how many people provide care to them. In the 1999-2000 sample, the number receiving care was lower than the number

providing care (3,029 and 5,065 respectively). This is because many recipients of care received help from more than one person within their household – each of whom was recorded as a separate carer.

Tables 6.4 and 6.6 show the main source of income received by the household in which the carer and the person being cared for live respectively. "Main source" is calculated as the category of income that gives the highest amount, and results should be interpreted with caution since some households may have more than one source that provides similar proportions.

Comparisons of earlier years' FRS data with the General Household Survey's (GHS) modules on informal care suggest that the FRS under reports both those receiving and those giving care. This is particularly where care is required less frequently and may be accounted for by the way the questions are asked. On the FRS, questions are asked as part of the household schedule, and, unlike the GHS, it is not always the case that the person providing or giving the care is addressed directly. GHS data therefore provide a more complete picture of all types of informal care. Uses of FRS data, such as in the modelling of benefits such as Invalid Care Allowance, are applicable to those requiring more frequent caring.

It should also be noted that the FRS does not record information on individuals in retirement or nursing homes. This means that figures relating to the most elderly individuals may not be representative of the Great Britain population, as many of those who require care at this age will have moved into homes where they can receive more frequent help.

Key definitions used
(for a full explanation of all definitions please refer to the Glossary)

- Informal carers
- Employment status
- Gross weekly household income

Changes to tables between 1998-1999 and 1999-2000

From 1999-2000 the questions on hours spent caring have been changed to record banded hours rather than an exact figure. When more than one person is cared for, the total banded hours is calculated using the midpoints. This change affects tables 6.1 and 6.4.

Previous year's tables 6.5, 6.6 and 6.8 have been removed from the publication as the questions on 'How long help has been received for' and 'What type of help' are no longer asked.

Table 6.1: Informal carers by sex, age and number of hours per week providing care

Percentage of informal carers

	Number of hours per week										
Informal carers	Less than 5	5 to less than 10	10 to less than 20	20 to less than 35	35 to less than 50	50 or more	Varies: Less than 35	Varies: 35 or more	Undefined	Total informal carers (base =100%)	Total individuals
Male											
4 and under	0	0	0	0	0	0	0	0	0	0	2,089
5 to 10	.	.	.	.	.	.	.	.	.	7	2,695
11 to 15	42	16	3	13	7	4	10	6	0	33	2,139
16 to 24	32	28	11	6	2	4	12	4	0	83	2,651
25 to 34	37	19	12	10	4	5	3	10	1	152	3,747
35 to 44	37	21	15	7	5	2	4	9	1	294	4,136
45 to 54	40	18	13	7	4	5	4	8	0	427	3,747
55 to 59	33	17	14	9	4	6	5	13	0	215	1,536
60 to 64	24	19	15	10	5	4	2	21	0	199	1,477
65 to 74	27	13	12	11	7	6	5	18	0	315	2,526
75 to 84	23	17	11	8	3	8	4	25	1	151	1,341
85 or over	.	.	.	.	.	.	.	.	.	13	275
Total male informal carers	33	18	13	9	5	5	5	13	-	1,889	28,359
Female											
4 and under	.	.	.	.	.	.	.	.	.	1	1,989
5 to 10	.	.	.	.	.	.	.	.	.	8	2,514
11 to 15	36	16	16	13	5	2	8	4	0	42	2,038
16 to 24	33	20	12	11	5	3	8	8	1	148	2,870
25 to 34	33	21	14	6	5	6	4	11	1	383	4,225
35 to 44	30	19	15	7	6	7	4	12	-	594	4,521
45 to 54	33	19	17	9	3	5	4	10	0	746	3,931
55 to 59	31	18	16	8	6	6	3	13	0	370	1,634
60 to 64	24	20	16	8	4	5	4	18	-	319	1,669
65 to 74	32	18	15	7	3	5	4	16	0	393	2,814
75 to 84	39	17	10	7	2	4	7	12	0	158	1,926
85 or over	.	.	.	.	.	.	.	.	.	14	520
Total female informal carers	31	19	15	8	4	5	4	12	-	3,176	30,651
Total informal carers											
4 and under	.	.	.	.	.	.	.	.	.	1	4,078
5 to 10	.	.	.	.	.	.	.	.	.	15	5,209
11 to 15	38	16	10	13	6	3	9	5	0	75	4,177
16 to 24	33	23	11	9	4	3	9	6	-	231	5,521
25 to 34	34	20	14	7	5	6	3	11	1	535	7,972
35 to 44	32	20	15	7	6	5	4	11	1	888	8,657
45 to 54	35	19	15	8	4	5	4	9	0	1,173	7,678
55 to 59	31	18	15	9	5	6	3	13	0	585	3,170
60 to 64	24	19	16	9	4	5	3	19	-	518	3,146
65 to 74	30	16	14	9	5	5	4	17	0	708	5,340
75 to 84	31	17	10	8	3	6	6	19	-	309	3,267
85 or over	.	.	.	.	.	.	.	.	.	27	795
Total informal carers	32	19	14	8	5	5	4	13	-	5,065	59,010

Table 6.2: Informal carers by relationship to person being cared for and whether living in or outside the household

Person being cared for	Informal Carers		Total informal carers
	Male	Female	
Household member			
Parent	6	8	7
Partner/spouse/cohabitee	23	15	18
Son/Daughter	7	5	6
Brother/Sister	2	1	1
Other relative	2	1	1
Non relative	1	-	1
Non household member			
Relative	36	40	39
Friend/neighbour	7	9	8
Client of voluntary organisation	8	11	10
Other non-household	1	1	1
More than one person cared for	8	7	8
Total informal carers (base = 100%)	1,889	3,176	5,065

Table 6.3: Adult informal carers by employment status and sex

Percentage of adults

Employment status	Adult informal carers			All adults		
	Male	Female	Total adult informal carers	Male	Female	Total adults
Employees						
full time	39	22	**28**	52	28	**40**
part time	5	22	**15**	4	19	**12**
Self employed						
full time	8	2	**4**	9	2	**5**
part time	1	2	**2**	1	2	**2**
ILO unemployed	4	2	**3**	5	2	**4**
Retired	24	20	**22**	17	24	**20**
Permanently sick or disabled	8	5	**6**	7	5	**6**
Other inactive	12	24	**20**	5	17	**11**
Total adults (base = 100%)	1,829	3,102	**4,931**	20,729	23,378	**44,107**

DSS, Family Resources Survey Great Britain 1999-2000, © Crown Copyright 2001

Table 6.4: Informal carers by sex, main source of gross weekly household income and hours caring

	Number of hours per week										
Main source of household income	Less than 5	5 to less than 10	10 to less than 20	20 to less than 35	35 to less than 50	50 or more	Varies: Less than 35	Varies: 35 or more	Undefined	Total informal carers	Total individuals
Male											
Wages and salaries	63	54	46	47	24	34	54	18	.	48	61
Self employment income	8	6	7	4	5	2	4	3	.	6	8
Investments	1	2	1	1	1	0	0	0	.	1	1
Retirement Pension plus any IS	9	13	15	15	25	26	18	30	.	16	8
Other pensions	10	9	11	11	7	7	8	12	.	10	6
Social Security disability benefits	3	6	9	10	15	17	4	16	.	8	3
Other Social Security benefits	6	9	11	11	22	14	12	19	.	11	11
Other sources	-	1	1	2	1	0	0	1	.	1	2
Total male informal carers (base=100%)	**628**	**343**	**248**	**159**	**89**	**91**	**85**	**242**	**4**	**1,889**	**28,359**
Female											
Wages and salaries	59	53	48	45	40	31	45	25	.	48	55
Self employment income	7	7	7	4	4	5	5	3	.	6	7
Investments	1	1	2	0	1	1	2	-	.	1	1
Retirement Pension plus any IS	12	14	12	15	16	19	18	21	.	15	13
Other pensions	11	9	10	6	8	4	8	10	.	9	6
Social Security disability benefits	2	4	8	11	10	16	10	18	.	8	3
Other Social Security benefits	7	10	12	18	21	24	13	21	.	13	13
Other sources	1	1	1	1	1	1	0	1	.	1	2
Total female informal carers (base=100%)	**997**	**618**	**483**	**246**	**141**	**168**	**132**	**385**	**6**	**3,176**	**30,651**
Total informal carers											
Wages and salaries	61	53	48	46	33	32	48	22	.	48	58
Self employment income	7	7	7	4	4	4	5	3	.	6	7
Investments	1	2	2	-	1	-	1	-	.	1	1
Retirement Pension plus any IS	11	14	13	15	19	22	18	25	.	15	11
Other pensions	11	9	10	8	8	5	8	11	.	10	6
Social Security disability benefits	2	5	8	11	12	16	7	18	.	8	3
Other Social Security benefits	6	10	12	15	21	20	13	20	.	12	12
Other sources	1	1	1	1	1	1	0	1	.	1	2
Total informal carers (base=100%)	**1,625**	**961**	**731**	**405**	**230**	**259**	**217**	**627**	**10**	**5,065**	**59,010**

Table 6.5: Household members receiving care by sex, age and frequency of help

Age	Continuously	Several times a day	Once or twice a day	Several times a week	Once a week	All those receiving care (base=100%)
Male						
4 and under	.	.	.	.	.	24
5 to 10	74	21	2	2	2	57
11 to 15	51	36	11	0	2	40
16 to 24	51	25	6	18	0	31
25 to 34	40	23	15	12	11	63
35 to 44	31	25	15	22	6	84
45 to 54	31	20	19	19	10	141
55 to 59	28	31	27	9	4	83
60 to 64	29	26	23	16	7	120
65 to 74	29	30	19	14	8	236
75 to 84	28	21	21	16	15	243
85 or over	22	17	21	26	14	113
All males receiving care	**33**	**25**	**18**	**15**	**9**	**1,235**
Female						
4 and under	.	.	.	.	.	14
5 to 10	59	36	3	0	3	34
11 to 15	.	.	.	.	.	23
16 to 24	66	17	3	12	2	36
25 to 34	28	24	20	17	11	67
35 to 44	32	31	18	16	3	113
45 to 54	39	25	17	15	4	164
55 to 59	22	34	20	17	7	103
60 to 64	30	25	20	19	6	140
65 to 74	21	23	18	22	16	298
75 to 84	18	16	23	25	18	499
85 or over	15	20	21	27	17	303
All females receiving care	**25**	**22**	**19**	**21**	**12**	**1,794**
All individuals						
4 and under	60	35	3	3	0	38
5 to 10	68	26	2	1	2	91
11 to 15	55	32	8	2	2	63
16 to 24	59	21	4	15	1	67
25 to 34	35	23	17	14	11	130
35 to 44	32	29	17	19	5	197
45 to 54	35	23	18	17	7	305
55 to 59	25	33	24	13	6	186
60 to 64	29	26	21	18	6	260
65 to 74	24	26	19	19	13	534
75 to 84	21	17	22	22	17	742
85 or over	17	19	21	27	16	416
All those receiving care	**28**	**23**	**19**	**19**	**11**	**3,029**

DSS, Family Resources Survey Great Britain 1999-2000, © Crown Copyright 2001

Table 6.6: Household members receiving care by main source of gross weekly household income and sex

Percentage of individuals

Main source of household income	Individuals receiving care			All individuals		
	Male	Female	**All those receiving care**	Male	Female	**Total individuals**
Wages and salaries	18	18	**18**	61	55	**58**
Self employment income	2	2	**2**	8	7	**7**
Investments	1	1	**1**	1	1	**1**
Retirement Pension plus any IS	31	47	**40**	8	13	**11**
Other pensions	8	8	**8**	6	6	**6**
Social Security disability benefits	22	11	**15**	3	3	**3**
Other Social Security benefits	18	13	**15**	11	13	**12**
Other sources	1	1	**1**	2	2	**2**
Total individuals (base=100%)	**1,235**	**1,794**	**3,029**	**28,359**	**30,651**	**59,010**

DSS, Family Resources Survey Great Britain 1999-2000, © Crown Copyright 2001

Chapter 7

Occupation and employment

Introduction

The FRS asks a number of questions relating to income from jobs and the number of jobs held, from which the respondents' employment, economic, social and socio-economic status can be derived. For those respondents not working, questions are asked regarding why they are not working and how long it is since they last worked.

Contents and points to note when interpreting tables

Tables 7.1 to 7.3 analyse employment status by sex, age, ethnic group and then Government Office Region. The Glossary provides definitions for the categories of employment status used within the FRS. It should be noted that the FRS definitions for full time work, self employment and unemployment differ from those used within the HBAI report. The FRS definition for employment is based upon self assessment in contrast to the HBAI definition which is based upon working 31 hours or more a week. All individuals are classified as unemployed by HBAI if they are in receipt of Jobseeker's Allowance, even if they have undertaken unpaid work in a family business within the last seven days.

In line with ILO definitions, if someone is on a government training scheme for employment, is working unpaid or receives money for an odd job, they are classified as a working adult on the FRS. However, these people are not asked the social class question. This explains why there appears to be a large proportion of adults in Table 7.7 who fall into the 'not reported' social class. For the purpose of this table, all working adults not asked social class questions are put into this group.

For those adults described as 'other inactive' in Tables 7.1 to 7.3, further questions are asked to examine their reasons for not looking for work, the results of which are in Table 7.4. ILO unemployed adults in Tables 7.1 to 7.3 are asked further questions regarding the time since they were last in paid employment, with the results displayed in Table 7.5. Tables 7.4 and 7.5 have been categorised by age and sex to provide a more detailed analysis.

Table 7.6 examines those adults working, but not self employed, and in receipt of non-financial benefits from their employer. Table 7.7 analyses all working adults, including the self employed, in terms of their total hours worked.

Benefit units with children or child care costs by economic status are examined in Tables 7.8 to 7.10. Weekly cost of care, as a percentage of gross benefit unit income, is analysed in addition to weekly cost of child care. It should be noted that questions about child care costs in 1999-2000 were only asked of those in work. Therefore, it is expected that some economic status categories in Tables 7.8 and 7.9 show all zeros, for example, where the head or spouse is over 60. These categories are included for consistency with other tables. Since April 2000, the FRS has asked about child care costs of all those with some financial arrangement. These cases will be included in next year's reports.

Where the head or spouse is unemployed in a benefit unit, the time since the head was last in paid employment is analysed against their total savings in Table 7.11.

Table 7.12 shows pension provision and shows adults by employment status and age. This table is similar to one which was included in the 1994-95 FRS publication but was removed from subsequent years due to concerns about misreporting. However, recent comparisons show that, at a broad level, FRS pension provision data is comparable to other sources. It should be noted that the others below pension age category in this table includes those who are:

- ILO unemployed,
- looking after family/home,
- permanently or temporarily sick or disabled,
- and other inactive

but excludes students and the retired. This explains why the 'others below pension age' group is not as large as might be expected and why the total males, females and adults sample counts are smaller than those shown in Table 7.1.

Key definitions used
(for a full explanation of all definitions please refer to the Glossary)

- Economic status
- Employment status
- Gross weekly benefit unit income

Changes to tables between 1998-1999 and 1999-2000

The questions on travel to work have been rotated off the survey in 1999-2000 (see Introduction). This means that the following tables do not appear in this report, but will return next year:

Table 7.8 – Travelling to work: working adults by sex, distance, mode of transport and social class

Table 7.9 – Working adults' average weekly travel costs by sex and mode of transport

Table 7:10 – Working adults' average weekly travel costs as a percentage of gross weekly individual income by sex and social class

Adults between state pension age and 70 are now asked follow up questions if they are not working and not away from work. Previously they were automatically catergorised as retired. This change can be seen by the increases from last year in adults over pension age within the 'other' catergory.

DSS, Family Resources Survey Great Britain 1999–2000, © Crown Copyright 2001

Table 7.1: Adults by sex, employment status and age

Employment status	16 to 24	25 to 34	35 to 44	45 to 54	55 to 59	60 to 64	65 to 74	75 to 84	85 or over	Total adults
Male										
Employees										
full time	57	74	71	65	48	27	2	-	0	52
part time	10	3	2	3	4	6	4	2	-	4
Self employed										
full time	3	8	13	14	13	8	2	1	0	9
part time	1	1	1	1	2	3	4	1	0	1
All in employment										
full time	60	82	84	79	61	35	4	1	0	61
part time	11	4	3	4	7	9	7	2	-	5
ILO unemployed	12	6	5	3	3	3	-	0	0	5
Retired	0	0	0	1	6	20	81	97	100	17
Student	10	1	-	-	0	0	-	0	0	2
Looking after family/home	-	-	1	-	-	-	-	0	•0	-
Permanently sick or disabled	2	4	5	9	17	24	4	0	0	7
Temporarily sick or disabled	1	1	-	-	1	1	-	0	0	-
Other inactive	3	2	1	2	5	8	3	0	0	3
Total males										
(base=100%)	**1,944**	**3,747**	**4,136**	**3,747**	**1,536**	**1,477**	**2,526**	**1,341**	**275**	**20,729**
Female										
Employees										
full time	47	44	36	38	24	8	1	-	0	28
part time	15	21	31	28	25	14	3	1	0	19
Self employed										
full time	-	2	4	4	3	1	-	-	0	2
part time	1	2	3	3	3	2	1	0	0	2
All in employment										
full time	47	46	40	42	27	9	1	-	0	30
part time	16	23	34	31	28	16	4	1	0	21
ILO unemployed	7	3	3	2	1	-	-	0	0	2
Retired	0	0	-	1	9	47	83	99	100	24
Student	11	2	1	-	0	-	0	0	0	2
Looking after family/home	11	19	14	7	9	7	4	0	0	10
Permanently sick or disabled	2	3	5	9	15	11	4	0	0	5
Temporarily sick or disabled	1	-	1	1	1	-	0	0	0	-
Other inactive	5	4	4	6	10	9	4	0	0	5
Total females										
(base=100%)	**2,138**	**4,225**	**4,521**	**3,931**	**1,634**	**1,669**	**2,814**	**1,926**	**520**	**23,378**

DSS, Family Resources Survey Great Britain 1999-2000, © Crown Copyright 2001

Table 7.1: Continued

Employment status	16 to 24	25 to 34	35 to 44	45 to 54	55 to 59	60 to 64	65 to 74	75 to 84	85 or over	Total adults
Total adults										
Employees										
full time	52	59	53	51	36	17	1	-	0	**40**
part time	12	12	16	16	14	10	3	1	-	**12**
Self employed										
full time	2	5	8	9	8	5	1	-	0	**5**
part time	1	1	2	2	3	2	2	-	0	**2**
All in employment										
full time	54	64	62	60	44	22	2	-	0	**45**
part time	13	13	18	18	17	13	6	1	-	**13**
ILO unemployed	10	5	4	3	2	2	-	0	0	**4**
Retired	0	0	-	1	7	34	82	98	100	**20**
Student	11	1	-	-	0	-	-	0	0	**2**
Looking after family/home	5	10	8	4	4	4	2	0	0	**5**
Permanently sick or disabled	2	3	5	9	16	17	4	0	0	**6**
Temporarily sick or disabled	1	-	1	1	1	-	-	0	0	**-**
Other inactive	4	3	3	4	7	8	4	0	0	**4**
Total adults										
(base =100%)	4,082	7,972	8,657	7,678	3,170	3,146	5,340	3,267	795	**44,107**

DSS, Family Resources Survey Great Britain 1999-2000, © Crown Copyright 2001

Table 7.2: Adults by sex, employment status and ethnic group

Percentage of adults

Employment status	White	Black	Indian	Pakistani/ Bangladeshi	Other	Total adults
Male						
Employees						
full time	53	46	46	34	44	52
part time	4	5	9	9	6	4
Self employed						
full time	9	6	13	10	12	9
part time	2	1	1	1	1	1
All in employment						
full time	61	52	59	44	55	61
part time	5	7	9	10	6	5
ILO unemployed	4	13	6	12	7	5
Retired	17	10	8	7	6	17
Student	1	4	3	8	10	2
Looking after family/home	-	1	1	1	-	-
Permanently sick or disabled	7	9	8	10	6	7
Temporarily sick or disabled	-	1	1	1	1	-
Other inactive	3	4	3	6	7	3
Total males						
(base=100%)	**19,598**	**311**	**267**	**283**	**270**	**20,729**
Female						
Employees						
full time	28	40	34	10	33	28
part time	20	12	14	4	11	19
Self employed						
full time	2	2	4	1	3	2
part time	2	1	1	-	2	2
All in employment						
full time	30	42	39	11	35	30
part time	22	13	15	5	13	21
ILO unemployed	2	5	4	7	3	2
Retired	25	9	6	5	6	24
Student	1	4	4	4	9	2
Looking after family/home	9	14	19	49	21	10
Permanently sick or disabled	5	6	6	11	4	5
Temporarily sick or disabled	-	1	1	1	0	-
Other inactive	5	6	7	8	8	5
Total females						
(base=100%)	**22,158**	**344**	**268**	**290**	**318**	**23,378**

Percentage of adults

Ethnic group

Employment status	White	Black	Indian	Pakistani/ Bangladeshi	Other	Total adults
Total adults						
Employees						
full time	40	43	40	22	38	40
part time	12	9	11	7	9	12
Self employed						
full time	5	4	9	6	7	5
part time	2	1	1	1	1	2
All in employment						
full time	45	47	49	28	45	45
part time	14	10	12	8	10	13
ILO unemployed	3	9	5	10	5	4
Retired	21	9	7	6	6	20
Student	1	4	4	6	10	2
Looking after family/home	5	8	10	25	11	5
Permanently sick or disabled	6	8	7	11	5	6
Temporarily sick or disabled	-	1	1	1	-	-
Other inactive	4	5	5	7	8	4
Total adults						
(base=100%)	41,756	655	535	573	588	44,107

DSS, Family Resources Survey Great Britain 1999-2000, © Crown Copyright 2001

Table 7.3: Adults by sex, employment status and region

Percentage of adults

Employment status	North East	North West and Merseyside	Yorkshire and the Humber	East Midlands	West Midlands	Eastern
Male						
Employees						
full time	48	52	50	56	54	54
part time	3	4	4	4	3	3
Self employed						
full time	7	7	8	8	8	12
part time	1	1	1	1	1	2
All in employment						
full time	54	59	58	63	62	65
part time	4	5	5	5	5	5
ILO unemployed	5	5	6	3	4	4
Retired	17	17	16	17	17	18
Student	-	2	2	1	2	1
Looking after family/home	1	-	-	-	-	-
Permanently sick or disabled	12	10	9	6	7	5
Temporarily sick or disabled	1	-	-	1	-	-
Other inactive	5	2	3	3	2	2
Total males						
(base=100%)	**1,029**	**2,524**	**1,827**	**1,561**	**1,889**	**2,076**
Female						
Employees						
full time	24	29	26	29	27	28
part time	20	19	21	20	21	20
Self employed						
full time	1	2	2	3	2	2
part time	1	2	1	2	1	2
All in employment						
full time	25	30	28	31	29	31
part time	21	20	23	22	22	22
ILO unemployed	4	2	2	3	2	2
Retired	23	25	23	24	25	25
Student	1	1	1	2	2	1
Looking after family/home	10	10	11	8	9	11
Permanently sick or disabled	8	6	6	5	5	3
Temporarily sick or disabled	1	-	-	-	-	-
Other inactive	6	5	5	4	4	4
Total females						
(base=100%)	**1,184**	**2,898**	**2,081**	**1,673**	**2,094**	**2,253**

Percentage of adults

Government Office Region

Employment status	London	South East	South West	England	Wales	Scotland	Great Britain
Male							
Employees							
full time	50	57	49	52	47	51	52
part time	5	4	5	4	3	4	4
Self employed							
full time	11	10	11	9	8	6	9
part time	2	2	2	2	2	1	1
All in employment							
full time	61	67	59	62	55	57	61
part time	6	6	8	5	5	5	5
ILO unemployed	5	3	3	4	5	8	5
Retired	13	17	20	17	18	15	17
Student	3	1	1	2	2	2	2
Looking after family/home	-	-	-	-	-	-	-
Permanently sick or disabled	6	4	6	7	11	10	7
Temporarily sick or disabled	-	-	-	-	-	1	-
Other inactive	3	2	2	3	4	3	3
Total males							
(base=100%)	**2,188**	**3,005**	**1,786**	**17,885**	**1,144**	**1,700**	**20,729**
Female							
Employees							
full time	32	31	24	29	23	29	28
part time	14	20	21	19	17	19	19
Self employed							
full time	2	3	3	2	2	1	2
part time	2	3	3	2	1	2	2
All in employment							
full time	35	34	27	31	26	30	30
part time	16	23	24	21	18	20	21
ILO unemployed	3	2	2	2	2	3	2
Retired	19	24	28	24	28	24	24
Student	3	1	1	1	3	2	2
Looking after family/home	15	8	9	10	9	8	10
Permanently sick or disabled	4	4	4	5	9	8	5
Temporarily sick or disabled	-	-	-	-	1	-	-
Other inactive	5	4	5	5	6	5	5
Total females							
(base=100%)	**2,452**	**3,330**	**2,060**	**20,025**	**1,306**	**2,047**	**23,378**

DSS, Family Resources Survey Great Britain 1999-2000, © Crown Copyright 2001

Table 7.3: Continued

Percentage of adults

Employment status	Government Office Region: North East	North West and Merseyside	Yorkshire and the Humber	East Midlands	West Midlands	Eastern
Total adults						
Employees						
full time	35	40	38	42	41	41
part time	12	12	13	12	12	12
Self employed						
full time	4	4	5	5	5	7
part time	1	1	1	2	1	2
All in employment						
full time	39	44	43	47	45	48
part time	13	13	14	14	14	14
ILO unemployed	4	4	4	3	3	3
Retired	21	21	20	21	21	22
Student	1	1	2	1	2	1
Looking after family/home	6	5	6	4	5	6
Permanently sick or disabled	10	8	7	6	6	4
Temporarily sick or disabled	1	-	-	-	-	-
Other inactive	6	3	4	4	3	3
Total adults (base=100%)	**2,213**	**5,422**	**3,908**	**3,234**	**3,983**	**4,329**

Percentage of adults

Government Office Region

Employment status	London	South East	South West	England	Wales	Scotland	**Great Britain**
Total adults							
Employees							
full time	41	44	36	40	35	39	**40**
part time	9	12	13	12	10	12	**12**
Self employed							
full time	7	6	7	6	5	4	**5**
part time	2	2	3	2	2	1	**2**
All in employment							
full time	48	50	43	46	40	43	**45**
part time	11	15	16	14	12	13	**13**
ILO unemployed	4	3	3	3	3	5	**4**
Retired	16	20	24	20	23	19	**20**
Student	3	1	1	2	2	2	**2**
Looking after family/home	8	4	5	5	5	4	**5**
Permanently sick or disabled	5	4	5	6	10	9	**6**
Temporarily sick or disabled	-	-	-	-	1	1	**-**
Other inactive	4	3	4	4	5	4	**4**
Total adults							
(base=100%)	**4,640**	**6,335**	**3,846**	**37,910**	**2,450**	**3,747**	**44,107**

Table 7.4: Adults classified as other inactive by sex, age and reason not looking for employment

Percentage of inactive adults

Reason not looking for employment	Age						Total adults
	16 to 24	25 to 34	35 to 44	45 to 54	55 to 59	60 to 64	
Male							
Believes no jobs are available	5	2	2	3	13	24	9
Not yet started looking	13	3	3	4	4	4	5
Does not need employment	0	2	4	13	15	9	7
Any other reason	52	77	78	74	59	61	66
Not reported	31	16	12	7	9	2	12
Total inactive males (base=100%)	**66**	**70**	**58**	**84**	**74**	**113**	**465**
Female							
Believes no jobs are available	0	2	3	3	4	0	4
Not yet started looking	8	2	2	4	4	0	4
Does not need employment	0	2	9	21	30	0	14
Any other reason	65	73	72	70	61	0	69
Not reported	27	22	14	2	2	0	10
Total inactive females (base=100%)	**97**	**159**	**169**	**231**	**164**	**148**	**968**
Total adults							
Believes no jobs are available	2	2	3	3	7	16	6
Not yet started looking	10	2	3	4	4	3	4
Does not need employment	0	2	8	19	25	13	12
Any other reason	59	74	73	71	60	67	68
Not reported	28	20	14	3	5	1	11
Total inactive adults (base=100%)	**163**	**229**	**227**	**315**	**238**	**261**	**1,433**

Table 7.5: Unemployed adults by sex, length of time since last in paid employment and age

Time since last employed	Age						Total
	16 to 24	25 to 34	35 to 44	45 to 54	55 to 59	60 or over	adults
Male							
Never worked	42	8	5	2	0	0	16
Less than 6 months	29	30	27	34	22	25	29
6 months and less than 1 year	9	15	12	12	12	15	12
1 year and less than 2 years	11	17	12	14	7	15	13
2 years and less than 5 years	4	17	15	12	19	25	12
5 years or more	0	5	10	8	9	11	5
Not reported	6	8	19	19	32	9	13
Total unemployed male adults (base=100%)	234	207	186	130	52	48	857
Female							
Never worked	42	10	8	7	.	.	19
Less than 6 months	28	25	20	18	.	.	23
6 months and less than 1 year	9	13	13	14	.	.	12
1 year and less than 2 years	12	15	7	12	.	.	11
2 years and less than 5 years	5	17	18	13	.	.	13
5 years or more	2	8	7	6	.	.	6
Not reported	3	12	27	30	.	.	16
Total unemployed female adults (base=100%)	155	146	124	102	24	10	561
Total adults							
Never worked	42	8	6	4	1	0	17
Less than 6 months	29	28	25	27	20	22	27
6 months and less than 1 year	9	14	13	13	13	12	12
1 year and less than 2 years	11	16	10	13	6	15	12
2 years and less than 5 years	4	17	16	12	20	26	13
5 years or more	1	6	9	7	11	11	5
Not reported	5	10	22	24	28	14	14
Total unemployed adults (base=100%)	389	353	310	232	76	58	1,418

DSS, Family Resources Survey Great Britain 1999-2000, © Crown Copyright 2001

Table 7.6: Employers' packages: employees by type of allowance or benefit and sex

Percentage of employees

Employers' package	Sex		Total employees
	Male	Female	
Childcare provisions/vouchers	-	-	-
Mileage allowances	3	2	3
Refunds of motoring expenses	1	1	1
Refunds of household expenditure	1	-	1
Luncheon Vouchers	1	1	1
Free or subsidised meals/canteen	18	17	18
Free or subsidised goods	5	6	6
Free or subsidised medical insurance	9	4	7
Shares or share options	8	5	7
Payment of school fees	-	-	-
Any allowance/benefit	33	29	31
No allowances/benefits in kind	67	71	69
Total employees (base=100%)	**11,251**	**10,869**	**22,120**

Table 7.7: Working adults by employment status, sex, total hours worked and social class

Percentage of working employee adults

| | | Social class | | | | | | | |
Hours worked	Professional	Managerial and technical	Non-manual skilled	Manual skilled	Partly skilled	Unskilled	Armed Forces	Not recorded	Total
Male employees									
Less than 16	1	1	4	1	5	8	2	100	**3**
16 and less than 31	3	3	8	4	8	11	2	0	**5**
31 and less than 41	32	28	44	31	37	38	42	0	**33**
41 and less than 51	43	41	35	43	35	31	29	0	**39**
51 and less than 61	13	19	8	16	11	10	13	0	**14**
61 or over	8	8	2	5	4	3	12	0	**6**
Total male employees (base=100%)	**844**	**3,684**	**1,401**	**3,157**	**1,553**	**437**	**67**	**108**	**11,251**
Female employees									
Less than 16	3	4	11	9	18	43	.	100	**12**
16 and less than 31	8	18	30	29	36	40	.	0	**27**
31 and less than 41	35	36	44	38	31	12	.	0	**37**
41 and less than 51	36	32	13	18	12	3	.	0	**19**
51 and less than 61	11	8	1	5	3	1	.	0	**4**
61 or over	7	2	-	1	1	-	.	0	**1**
Total female employees (base=100%)	**305**	**3,298**	**4,049**	**744**	**1,808**	**584**	**1**	**80**	**10,869**
All employees									
Less than 16	2	3	9	2	12	27	2	100	**8**
16 and less than 31	4	10	24	8	22	27	2	0	**15**
31 and less than 41	32	32	44	33	34	24	42	0	**35**
41 and less than 51	41	37	19	39	23	16	30	0	**30**
51 and less than 61	13	14	3	14	7	5	13	0	**9**
61 or over	8	5	1	4	2	1	12	0	**4**
Total employees (base=100%)	**1,149**	**6,982**	**5,450**	**3,901**	**3,361**	**1,021**	**68**	**188**	**22,120**

DSS, Family Resources Survey Great Britain 1999-2000, © Crown Copyright 2001

Table 7.7: Continued

Hours worked	Professional	Managerial and technical	Non-manual skilled	Manual skilled	Partly skilled	Unskilled	Armed Forces	Not recorded	**Total**
Male self employed									
Less than 16	9	7	10	3	5	9	0	100	**9**
16 and less than 31	8	13	10	7	10	16	0	0	**10**
31 and less than 41	19	16	23	26	35	32	0	0	**22**
41 and less than 51	29	20	28	32	28	26	0	0	**26**
51 and less than 61	19	18	15	20	13	10	0	0	**17**
61 or over	16	25	14	12	9	8	0	0	**16**
Total male self employed									
(base=100%)	**256**	**635**	**183**	**771**	**192**	**73**	**0**	**62**	**2,172**
Female self employed									
Less than 16	7	17	25	19	18	72	0	100	**30**
16 and less than 31	28	23	27	30	31	21	0	0	**23**
31 and less than 41	21	19	24	23	21	4	0	0	**18**
41 and less than 51	27	17	10	14	21	0	0	0	**14**
51 and less than 61	12	13	7	5	6	2	0	0	**8**
61 or over	5	11	7	10	3	0	0	0	**7**
Total female self employed									
(base=100%)	**59**	**364**	**207**	**39**	**137**	**40**	**0**	**109**	**955**
All self employed									
Less than 16	9	11	18	3	10	31	0	100	**15**
16 and less than 31	11	17	19	8	18	18	0	0	**13**
31 and less than 41	19	17	23	26	30	22	0	0	**21**
41 and less than 51	29	19	19	31	25	17	0	0	**23**
51 and less than 61	18	16	11	19	10	7	0	0	**15**
61 or over	14	20	10	12	6	5	0	0	**13**
Total self employed									
(base=100%)	**315**	**999**	**390**	**810**	**329**	**113**	**0**	**171**	**3,127**

DSS, Family Resources Survey Great Britain 1999-2000, © Crown Copyright 2001

Percentage of working adults

Hours worked	Professional	Managerial and technical	Non-manual skilled	Manual skilled	Partly skilled	Unskilled	Armed Forces	Not recorded	Total
Male working adults									
Less than 16	3	2	4	1	5	8	2	100	4
16 and less than 31	4	4	8	4	8	12	2	0	6
31 and less than 41	29	27	41	30	36	37	42	0	31
41 and less than 51	40	38	34	41	34	30	29	0	37
51 and less than 61	15	19	9	16	11	10	13	0	15
61 or over	9	11	4	6	5	4	12	0	7
Total male working adults (base=100%)	1,100	4,319	1,584	3,928	1,745	510	67	170	13,423
Female working adults									
Less than 16	3	6	12	10	18	45	.	100	14
16 and less than 31	11	18	30	29	36	39	.	0	27
31 and less than 41	33	34	43	38	30	12	.	0	35
41 and less than 51	34	30	13	18	12	3	.	0	18
51 and less than 61	11	9	2	5	3	1	.	0	4
61 or over	7	3	1	1	1	-	.	0	1
Total female working adults (base=100%)	364	3,662	4,256	783	1,945	624	1	189	11,824
All working adults									
Less than 16	3	4	10	2	11	27	2	100	8
16 and less than 31	6	10	24	8	22	26	2	0	15
31 and less than 41	30	30	42	32	33	24	42	0	33
41 and less than 51	38	35	19	38	23	16	30	0	29
51 and less than 61	14	14	4	15	7	5	13	0	10
61 or over	9	7	1	6	3	2	12	0	5
Total working adults (base=100%)	1,464	7,981	5,840	4,711	3,690	1,134	68	359	25,247

DSS, Family Resources Survey Great Britain 1999-2000, © Crown Copyright 2001

Table 7.8: Benefit units with child care costs by economic status

Percentage of benefit units with child care costs

Weekly costs of childcare	Self employed	Single or couple, all in full time work	Couple, one in full time work, one in part time work	Couple, one in full time work, one not working	One or more in part time work
Term time costs					
Less than £10	4	2	13	10	15
£10 but less than £20	13	12	18	11	27
£20 but less than £30	12	13	15	16	18
£30 but less than £40	6	12	8	9	9
£40 but less than £50	7	11	11	14	6
£50 but less than £60	7	7	8	7	9
£60 but less than £70	7	6	7	15	6
£70 but less than £80	2	6	4	0	2
£80 or more	43	31	16	18	8
Total with child care costs (base=100%)	100	438	291	46	94
Total benefit units with children	920	1,543	1,834	1,294	779
Holidays					
Less than £10	1	1	5	0	13
£10 but less than £20	8	5	10	11	13
£20 but less than £30	6	8	12	4	19
£30 but less than £40	8	7	10	17	13
£40 but less than £50	8	9	16	14	6
£50 but less than £60	8	10	13	18	12
£60 but less than £70	11	6	7	13	10
£70 but less than £80	3	9	5	3	2
£80 or more	48	45	22	19	13
Total with child care costs (base=100%)	94	383	257	29	89
Total benefit units with children	920	1,543	1,834	1,294	779

DSS, Family Resources Survey Great Britain 1999-2000, © Crown Copyright 2001

Table 7.8: Continued

Weekly costs of childcare	Head or spouse aged 60 or over	Head or spouse unemployed	Head or spouse sick or disabled	Others	Total benefit units
Term time costs					
Less than £10	0	0	.	.	7
£10 but less than £20	0	0	.	.	15
£20 but less than £30	0	0	.	.	14
£30 but less than £40	0	0	.	.	10
£40 but less than £50	0	0	.	.	10
£50 but less than £60	0	0	.	.	8
£60 but less than £70	0	0	.	.	7
£70 but less than £80	0	0	.	.	4
£80 or more	0	0	.	.	25
Total with child care costs (base=100%)	0	0	1	4	974
Total benefit units with children	19	305	541	758	7,993
Holidays					
Less than £10	0	0	.	.	3
£10 but less than £20	0	0	.	.	8
£20 but less than £30	0	0	.	.	10
£30 but less than £40	0	0	.	.	9
£40 but less than £50	0	0	.	.	11
£50 but less than £60	0	0	.	.	11
£60 but less than £70	0	0	.	.	8
£70 but less than £80	0	0	.	.	6
£80 or more	0	0	.	.	34
Total with child care costs (base=100%)	0	0	1	3	856
Total benefit units with children	19	305	541	758	7,993

DSS, Family Resources Survey Great Britain 1999-2000, © Crown Copyright 2001

Table 7.9: Benefit units with child care costs by weekly cost as a percentage of gross weekly benefit unit income and economic status

Percentage of benefit units with child care costs

			Economic status		
Percentage of gross income	Self employed	Single or couple, all in full time work	Couple, one in full time work, one in part time work	Couple, one in full time work, one not working	One or more in part time work
Term time					
More than 0 but less than 10%	66	70	82	63	55
10 but less than 20%	23	25	17	24	30
20 but less than 30%	10	4	1	8	9
30 but less than 40%	1	-	-	2	2
40 but less than 50%	0	0	0	0	1
50% or more	0	-	0	2	1
Undefined	0	0	0	0	0
Total with child care costs (base=100%)	**100**	**438**	**291**	**46**	**94**
Holidays					
More than 0 but less than 10%	53	57	76	59	40
10 but less than 20%	31	32	22	24	37
20 but less than 30%	11	8	1	10	14
30 but less than 40%	2	3	1	3	6
40 but less than 50%	1	0	0	0	3
50% or more	1	1	0	3	1
Undefined	0	0	0	0	0
Total with child care costs (base=100%)	**94**	**383**	**257**	**29**	**89**

Table 7.9: Continued

Percentage of gross income	Economic status				Total benefit units
	Head or spouse aged 60 or over	Head or spouse unemployed	Head or spouse sick or disabled	Others	
Term time					
More than 0 but less than 10%	0	0	.	.	71
10 but less than 20%	0	0	.	.	23
20 but less than 30%	0	0	.	.	5
30 but less than 40%	0	0	.	.	1
40 but less than 50%	0	0	.	.	-
50% or more	0	0	.	.	-
Undefined	0	0	.	.	0
Total with child care costs (base=100%)	**0**	**0**	**1**	**4**	**974**
Holidays					
More than 0 but less than 10%	0	0	.	.	60
10 but less than 20%	0	0	.	.	29
20 but less than 30%	0	0	.	.	7
30 but less than 40%	0	0	.	.	2
40 but less than 50%	0	0	.	.	-
50% or more	0	0	.	.	1
Undefined	0	0	.	.	0
Total with child care costs (base=100%)	**0**	**0**	**1**	**3**	**856**

DSS, Family Resources Survey Great Britain 1999-2000, © Crown Copyright 2001

Table 7.10: Benefit units with children by economic status and age of youngest child

Percentage of benefit units with children

Economic status	4 and under	5 to 10	11 to 15	16 to 19	Total
Couples with children					
Self employed	13	16	17	17	**15**
Single or couple, all in full time work	13	19	27	30	**19**
Couple, one in full time work,					
one in part time work	28	37	29	24	**31**
Couple, one in full time work,					
one not working	32	17	14	13	**22**
One or more in part time work	6	5	5	7	**5**
Head or spouse aged 60 or over	-	-	1	1	**-**
Head or spouse unemployed	4	2	2	1	**3**
Head or spouse sick or disabled	3	4	6	6	**4**
Others	1	-	-	1	**1**
Total couples with children					
(base=100%)	**2,450**	**1,718**	**1,252**	**442**	**5,862**
Singles with children					
Self employed	1	1	3	7	**2**
Single or couple, all in full time work	9	19	32	48	**20**
Couple, one in full time work,	0	0	0	0	**0**
one in part time work	0	0	0	0	**0**
Couple, one in full time work,	0	0	0	0	**0**
one not working	0	0	0	0	**0**
One or more in part time work	16	28	23	21	**22**
Head or spouse aged 60 or over	0	-	-	0	**-**
Head or spouse unemployed	6	6	8	7	**7**
Head or spouse sick or disabled	12	17	15	13	**15**
Others	57	28	18	4	**35**
Total singles with children					
(base=100%)	**763**	**719**	**482**	**167**	**2,131**

DSS, Family Resources Survey Great Britain 1999-2000, © Crown Copyright 2001

Table 7.11: Benefit units where head or spouse unemployed by type, amount of savings and length of time since last in paid employment

Percentage of unemployed, head or spouse, benefit units

Capital	Head currently in work	Head never worked	Less than 6 months	6 months and less than 1 year	1 year and less than 2 years	2 years and less than 5 years	5 years or more	Not reported	Total benefit units
					Time since head last in paid employment				
Couples									
No savings	.	.	69	68	77	75	.	77	**73**
Less than £1,500	.	.	16	18	3	14	.	12	**14**
£1,500 but less than £3,000	.	.	0	4	3	3	.	3	**3**
£3,000 but less than £8,000	.	.	4	8	6	0	.	8	**4**
£8,000 but less than £10,000	.	.	0	0	0	0	.	0	**0**
£10,000 but less than £16,000	.	.	0	3	0	0	.	0	**-**
£16,000 but less than £20,000	.	.	0	0	0	0	.	0	**0**
£20,000 or more	.	.	11	0	10	8	.	0	**5**
Total two adult (head or spouse unemployed) benefit units (base=100%)	7	19	62	33	29	34	21	37	**242**
Single adults									
No savings	.	79	71	77	69	78	75	77	**74**
Less than £1,500	.	14	17	16	22	15	23	17	**18**
£1,500 but less than £3,000	.	2	3	1	2	3	0	4	**3**
£3,000 but less than £8,000	.	3	4	4	6	2	1	1	**3**
£8,000 but less than £10,000	.	1	1	0	1	0	0	0	**1**
£10,000 but less than £16,000	.	1	1	0	1	1	0	0	**1**
£16,000 but less than £20,000	.	0	1	0	0	0	0	0	**-**
£20,000 or more	.	0	2	1	0	1	0	1	**1**
Total single adult (head unemployed) benefit units (base=100%)	19	199	197	89	111	99	48	145	**907**

DSS, Family Resources Survey Great Britain 1999-2000, © Crown Copyright 2001

Table 7.12: Pension provision: adults by employment status and age

Pension provision	16 to 24	25 to 34	35 to 44	45 to 54	55 to 59	60 to 64	65 or over	Total adults
Male								
Employees								
Occupational pension only	15	44	57	59	53	35	3	**46**
Personal pension only	4	15	15	15	14	13	1	**13**
Either occupational or personal pension or both	19	61	75	77	70	51	4	**61**
No pension scheme	81	39	25	23	30	49	96	**39**
Total male employees (base=100%)	**1,310**	**2,903**	**3,049**	**2,549**	**802**	**481**	**157**	**11,251**
Self employed								
Personal pension only	11	46	56	57	57	44	9	**48**
No pension scheme	89	54	44	43	43	56	91	**52**
Total male self employed (base=100%)	**88**	**347**	**584**	**579**	**238**	**170**	**166**	**2,172**
Others								
Personal pension only	0	2	3	3	2	2	1	**2**
No pension scheme	100	97	95	93	97	96	98	**96**
Total other males (base=100%)	**357**	**458**	**487**	**585**	**402**	**525**	**202**	**3,016**

Current pension provision only - excludes frozen pensions from earlier periods of employment.

Percentage of adults

Pension provision	16 to 24	25 to 34	35 to 44	45 to 54	55 to 59	60 to 64	65 or over	Total adults
				Age				
Female								
Employees								
Occupational pension only	19	48	49	49	45	30	2	**43**
Personal pension only	3	9	9	9	8	7	0	**8**
Either occupational or								
personal pension or both	22	58	59	60	55	37	2	**52**
No pension scheme	78	42	41	40	45	63	98	**48**
Total female employees								
(base=100%)	**1,295**	**2,710**	**2,998**	**2,593**	**781**	**361**	**131**	**10,869**
Self employed								
Personal pension only	5	31	33	38	20	16	0	**29**
No pension scheme	95	69	67	62	80	84	100	**71**
Total female self employed								
(base=100%)	**30**	**156**	**294**	**279**	**99**	**50**	**47**	**955**
Others								
Personal pension only	1	2	1	2	1	1	0	**2**
No pension scheme	99	96	98	96	97	98	100	**97**
Total other females								
(base=100%)	**610**	**1,295**	**1,201**	**1,000**	**600**	**446**	**318**	**5,470**

Current pension provision only - excludes frozen pensions from earlier periods of employment

DSS, Family Resources Survey Great Britain 1999-2000, © Crown Copyright 2001

Table 7.12: Continued

Pension provision	16 to 24	25 to 34	35 to 44	45 to 54	55 to 59	60 to 64	65 or over	Total adults
Total adults								
Employees								
Occupational pension only	17	46	53	54	49	33	2	**45**
Personal pension only	4	12	12	12	11	10	1	**11**
Either occupational or personal pension or both	20	59	68	69	63	45	3	**57**
No pension scheme	80	41	32	31	37	55	97	**43**
Total employees								
(base=100%)	**2,605**	**5,613**	**6,047**	**5,142**	**1,583**	**842**	**288**	**22,120**
Self employed								
Personal pension only	9	42	49	51	47	38	7	**43**
No pension provision	91	58	51	49	53	62	93	**57**
Total self employed								
(base=100%)	**118**	**503**	**878**	**858**	**337**	**220**	**213**	**3,127**
Others								
Personal pension only	-	2	2	3	1	2	-	**2**
No pension scheme	99	96	97	95	97	97	99	**97**
Total other adults								
(base=100%)	**967**	**1,753**	**1,688**	**1,585**	**1,002**	**971**	**520**	**8,486**

Current pension provision only - excludes frozen pensions from earlier periods of employment.

Methodology

Population

The Family Resources Survey sample aims to cover private households in Great Britain. Like some other household surveys, the area to the North of the Caledonian Canal and all of the Scottish Highlands and Islands are excluded due to disproportionate fieldwork costs in this area. This coverage excludes approximately three per cent of the delivery points (letterboxes) in Scotland, which equates to 0.25 per cent of delivery points in Great Britain.

Framework for sample selection

The FRS uses a stratified clustered probability sample drawn from the Royal Mail's small users Postcode Address File (PAF). The PAF is a list of all addresses where less than 50 items of mail are received a day, and is updated twice a year.

The survey selects 1,680 postcode sectors with a probability of selection that is proportional to size. Each sector is known as a Primary Sampling Unit (PSU).

The PSUs are stratified by 26 regions and also by three other variables derived from the 1991 Census of Population. Stratifying ensures that proportions of the sample falling into each group reflect those of the population.

Within each region the postcode sectors are ranked and grouped into six equal bands using the proportion of heads of household in socio-economic groups one to five or 13. Within each of these six bands, the PSUs are ranked by the adult economic activity rate and formed into three further bands, resulting in 18 bands for each region. These are then ranked according to the proportion of unemployed men. This set of stratifiers is chosen to have a maximum effectiveness on the accuracy of two key variables: household income and housing costs. The table below summarises the stratifiers.

Regions	19 in England (Metropolitan/ non-Metropolitan/4 in London)
	2 in Wales
	5 in Scotland
Socio-economic groups	1 Employers/Managers in large establishments
	2 Employers/Managers in small establishments
	3 Professional workers (self employed)
	4 Professional workers (employees)
	5 Non-manual ancillary workers, foremen and supervisors
	13 Farmers (employers and managers)
Economic activity rate	
Male unemployment	

Within each PSU a sample of addresses is selected. In 1999-2000, 25 addresses were selected per PSU. This means that nationally there was approximately a one in 571 chance of an address being selected.

Each year, one half of the PSUs are retained from the previous year's sample, but with new addresses chosen; while for the other half of the sample, a fresh selection of PSUs is made (which in turn will be retained for the following year). This is to improve comparability between years.

Data collection methods

The Consortium of Social Survey Division (SSD) of the Office for National Statistics and the National Centre for Social Research (formerly SCPR) have been conducting fieldwork for the FRS since 1992. In September 1996 and September

2000 the FRS contract was tendered as part of the good practice in government programme. The consortium were successful both times and currently hold the contract until 2004 with the option of a two year extension.

Interviews are carried out jointly on behalf of the DSS by interviewers from the Office for National Statistics and the National Centre for Social Research. Each month the PSUs are systematically divided between the two organisations and then assigned to the field staff.

Before interviewers make contact with the selected addresses, a letter is sent to the address, explaining that it has been chosen for the survey, and that an interviewer will call. Participation in the FRS is voluntary. In October 1997 the FRS advance letter was revised following methodological work carried out by the Office for National Statistics and also a split sample test conducted jointly by the Office for National Statistics and SCPR on the FRS. The letter was simplified and its length reduced.

The interviewers are asked to call at the address. A lower limit of four calls is set and these calls have to be made at different times of the day and on different days of the week. In 1999-2000, FRS interviewers averaged 7.7 calls per address before returning it as a non-contact.

The FRS was one of the first Government surveys to use Computer Assisted Personal Interviewing (CAPI). There are advantages to this over the traditional paper interviews, primarily:

- in-built checks for consistency can be made at the time of the interview,
- respondents are automatically routed only to those questions relevant to them,
- there is no need for a data input stage as the data are already available,
- questions with alternate wordings (eg is/was, his/her) can be automatically tailored to the situation,
- interviewers receive and transmit work via a modem in their own homes.

The average (mean) interview length is around one hour and 20 minutes, but the time will vary according to the size of household and its circumstances. The most common length of interview was recorded at sixty minutes.

The questionnaire itself is divided into three parts. First, the household schedule which is addressed to one person in the household (usually the head, although other members are encouraged to be present) and which mainly asks household level information, such as relationship of individuals to each other, tenure and housing costs. Second, the individual schedule which is addressed to each adult in turn and asks questions about employment, benefits, pensions, investments and other income. A final section goes on to ask the value of investments for relevant respondents.

To contain the length of the overall questionnaire, and to reduce the respondent burden of an overlong interview, FRS users have agreed to rotate off blocks of questions. 'Rotated' sections of the questionnaire will be asked every other year, rather than every year. This can often still yield enough data for useful analysis.

Rotated off for 1999-2000 are "NHS treatment" and "Travel to work".

Rotated off for 2000-2001 will be "Vehicle ownership" and "Household Durables".

Interviewers new to the FRS are briefed on the questionnaire and an annual re-briefing is given to all interviewers on changes to the questionnaire. Those who have been working on the survey for some time also complete a written field report each year, describing their experiences with particular parts of the questionnaire, and commenting on how changes are received in the field.

Consultation of documentation

Interviewers are encouraged to consult documentation from respondents at all stages of the interview to ensure that the data are as accurate as possible. For some items, whether or not certain documents are consulted is recorded on the questionnaire, helping users of the data to judge the accuracy.

Of all employees interviewed in 1999-2000, 54 per cent consulted a payslip in order to answer questions on the income from their employment. However, it should be noted that eight per cent of employees simply did not have a payslip to consult.

In recording data on benefit receipt, some form of documentation (an order book, a letter from the DSS or Benefits Agency or a bank statement) was consulted for 67 per cent of all benefits received.

The questionnaire records consultation of documentation for questions relating to Council Tax. 48 per cent of households consulted a Council Tax bill or statement in answering questions on their Council Tax payments.

In addition, self-employed respondents are asked if they have documentation when they provide information about

Table 1: Response in the 1999-00 Family Resources Survey

	Number of households	Percentage of effective sample
Sampled addresses	42,472	
Ineligible addresses	4,602	
Effective sample (eligible households)	37,870	100
Fully co-operating households	24,988	66
Partially co-operating households	432	1
Refusals	10,819	29
Households with no contact	1,631	4

the profit or loss of their business. Of the 75 per cent of self employed respondents who had prepared business accounts, 31 per cent were able to refer to such documentation.

Response

The FRS aims to interview all adults in a household. A household is defined as fully co-operating when it meets this requirement. In addition, to count as fully co-operating, there must be less than 13 'don't know' or 'refusal' answers to monetary amount questions in the benefit unit schedule (i.e. excluding the assets section of the questionnaire). Proxy interviews are accepted only under restricted circumstances. In 1999-2000, for those households classed as fully co-operating, proxy responses were obtained for 15 per cent of adults.

If a household is partially co-operating, the minimum requirement is that a full interview has been obtained from the head of household's benefit unit.

It should be noted that all data shown in the main body of this publication refer to fully co-operating households.

Table 1 summarises the household response. The original sample chosen for 1999-2000 consisted of 42,472 addresses. However, 4,602 were then found to be ineligible because they were not defined as private households or were empty households. This left an effective sample of 37,870 households. Of these, 24,988 fully co-operated (66 per cent), 432 only partially co-operated (one per cent) and 10,819 refused to proceed with the interview (29 per cent). The interviewer was unable to make contact with 1,631 households (four per cent), the same proportion as in 1998-99.

The reasons for refusal and non-contact are recorded. The most common reason for refusal given was the feeling that answering questions from the FRS would an 'invasion of privacy' (17 per cent); followed by 14 per cent who said they 'couldn't be bothered' and 14 per cent who 'don't believe in surveys'. Concerns about confidentiality were only raised by four per cent of households. Six per cent said they 'disliked a survey of income'.

The main reason given for non-contact was that there was rarely anybody at the address (28 per cent). A further 11 per cent of households could not be contacted because of the working shifts or odd hours of people in the household.

The achieved sample size was 24,988 households.

Table 2 shows response rates broken down by Government Office Region. Response rates are calculated as follows:

$$\frac{\text{Number of fully co-operating households}}{\text{Number of eligible households}} \times 100$$

The overall response rate for the FRS for the year 1999-2000 was 66 per cent.

The region with the highest response rate was North East, where 72 per cent of all households selected responded fully, followed closely by Wales (71 per cent). The region with the lowest response rate was London where only 60 per cent of the chosen households fully co-operated. The variation in response rates reflects those of other major surveys including the Census of Population. That is that response rates are generally lower in large city areas.

Table 2: Regional response rates

Government Office Region	Percentage of households
North East	72
North West and Merseyside	67
Yorkshire and the Humber	67
East Midlands	66
West Midlands	64
Eastern	67
London	60
South East	66
South West	68
England	66
Wales	71
Scotland	65
Great Britain	**66**

Non-response

The lower the response rate to a survey, the greater the likelihood that those who responded are significantly unlike those who did not, and so the greater the risk of systematic bias in the survey results. Unless information is available about the nature and extent of such bias there are likely to be problems in generalising the sample results to the population. For a British survey of the size and complexity of the FRS the total non-response rate in 1999-2000 of 34 per cent is not considered unreasonable. However, any information that can be obtained about the non-responders is useful both in terms of future attempts to improve the overall response rate and also potentially in improving the weighting of the sample results. It is considered a priority issue for the FRS to obtain as much information as possible about non-responders. The following sections outline some of the analysis that has been carried out in this direction.

FRS non-response and ACORN classifications

A number of household characteristics are often associated with a higher or lower response rate on surveys[1]. Lower response rates than the average are often seen in:

- households in inner-city areas (especially London);
- single person households;
- head of household born outside the UK.

In contrast, higher response rates occur, for example, in households with dependent children. A greater understanding of how these varied characteristics interact and influence survey response can be useful for weighting of results and for maximising response rates in the future.

The DSS commissioned a study of non-response to the Family Resources Survey in relation to the ACORN[2] code of a household. ACORN is a geo-demographic classification system developed by CACI Marketing Systems. It is primarily aimed at identifying consumer markets by using data for Enumeration Districts from the 1991 Census. Clusters of Census data items such as age, sex, marital status, occupation, education, home ownership, car ownership, family structure and ethnic group are used to derive 54 ACORN 'types' which are amalgamated into 17 'groups' which in turn can be classified into six 'categories.' The various ACORN codes are accompanied by brief descriptions and pen portraits of the sort of households included in a particular code.

Tables 3 and 4 summarise the results of the analysis, showing the ACORN area 'types' with response rates significantly below or above the average for 1995-96 and 1995-96 and 1996-97 combined. The codes are numbered from one to 54 with the lower codes indicating the more prosperous areas. Table 3 shows that for the two years combined, eight of the 11 areas with a response rate significantly below average have ACORN codes from one to 27. The FRS appears to be under-representing wealthier households. Similarly, Table 4 shows that nine of the 14 areas with a response rate significantly above average are in the less prosperous half of the ACORN codes (a code of 28 or above). This suggests that the FRS is over-representing poorer households. However, as the tables show, the detailed ACORN 'types' do not differ by more than 10 per cent in either direction from the 1995-97 average of 69.5 per cent.

The relationship between non-response and ACORN classification was also carried out for the Family Expenditure Survey (FES) combining data from two survey years (1995-

---

[1] Kate Foster (1996) 'A comparison of Census characteristics of respondents and non-respondents to the 1991 Family Expenditure Survey', Survey Methodology Bulletin, 38, OPCS

[2] CACI Limited 1994. All rights reserved. Source: Office for National Statistics and GRO(s) Crown Copyright 1991. All rights reserved.

Table 3: ACORN [1] area 'Types' with a statistically significant lower than average response rate

| | Percentage response rate | | | | | | | |
| | Full (%) | | Partial (%) | | Refusal (%) | | Non-Contact (%) | |
ACORN Types	1995-96	1995-97	1995-96	1995-97	1995-96	1995-97	1995-96	1995-97
24 Partially gentrified multi-ethnic areas	60	60	3	3	29	30	8	7
21 Prosperous enclaves, highly qualified executives	61	61	4	3	23	25	13	11
47 Council estates with high unemployment	61	63	3	2	27	27	9	8
25 Converted flats & bedsits, single people	63	63	2	2	26	27	9	8
23 Affluent city centre areas, tenements & flats	64	63	0	0	26	27	11	9
9 Private flats, elderly people	65	65	0	0	29	30	5	5
1 Wealthy Suburbs, large detached houses	65	66	2	1	31	30	3	2
53 Multi ethnic, severe unemployment, lone parents	65	66	2	2	22	24	11	8
36 Home owning multi ethnic areas, young families	66	65	4	2	27	29	4	3
5 Mature, well-off suburbs	67	67	2	2	29	29	3	2
26 More established home owning areas	69	67	1	1	28	30	2	2

Table 4: ACORN [1] area 'Types' with a statistically significant higher than average response rate

| | Percentage response rate | | | | | | | |
| | Full (%) | | Partial (%) | | Refusal (%) | | Non-Contact (%) | |
ACORN Types	1995-96	1995-97	1995-96	1995-97	1995-96	1995-97	1995-96	1995-97
6 Agricultural villages, home-based workers	78	76	1	1	20	22	1	3
12 Transient workforces, living at their place of work	76	77	0	0	23	20	1	3
50 Council areas, high unemployment, lone parents	75	75	3	2	21	21	2	2
35 Low rise estates, older workers, new home owners	75	74	1	1	22	23	2	2
43 Council areas, young families, many lone parents	75	73	1	1	21	21	4	4
39 Home owners, small council flats, single pensioners	75	72	1	1	22	25	3	3
40 Council areas, older people, health problems	75	71	1	1	22	26	3	2
51 Council flats, greatest hardship, many lone parents	74	75	0	0	19	19	7	6
42 Council areas, young families, some new home owners	73	74	2	2	22	22	3	2
27 Rural areas, mixed occupations	73	73	2	1	23	23	2	2
41 Better off council areas, new home owners	73	72	2	1	22	24	3	3
2 Villages with wealthy commuters	73	71	1	1	24	24	2	3
4 Affluent suburbs, older families	73	70	1	1	24	27	2	2
46 Council areas, residents with health problems	71	71	2	1	24	24	3	3

[1] CACI Limited 1994. All rights reserved.

Source: ONS and GRO(s) Crown Copyright 1991. All rights reserved.

Table 5: Response and non-response rates by selected ACORN[1] area 'Types': FES 1995-97 and FRS 1995-97

| | Percentage response rate | | | | | |
| | Full (%) | | Refusal (%) | | Non-Contact (%) | |
ACORN Types	FES	FRS	FES	FRS	FES	FRS
6 Agricultural villages, home-based workers	75	76	25	22	0	2
13 Home owning family areas	70	69	29	29	1	2
27 Rural areas, mixed occupations	72	73	27	28	1	2
32 Home owning areas, skilled workers	68	71	30	26	2	4
34 Mature home owning areas, skilled workers	67	68	31	30	1	2
41 Better-off Council, new home owners	69	72	30	25	1	3
44 Multi-occupied terraces, multi-ethnic	71	70	24	25	5	5
Areas with below-average response (FES)						
1 Wealthy suburbs, large detached houses	59	66	39	31	1	2
5 Mature, well-off suburbs	59	67	38	31	3	2
18 Furnished flats and bedsits, young singles	48	66	36	26	16	9
19 Apartments, young professionals	53	67	42	28	5	5
20 Gentrified multi-ethnic areas	55	55	55	26	8	5
21 Prosperous areas, highly qualified executives	51	61	38	28	12	11
47 Council estates, high unemployment	55	63	38	29	7	8
49 Council flats, very high unemployment, singles	58	72	33	20	10	7
53 Multi-ethnic, severe unemployment, lone parents	47	66	45	26	7	8

[1] CACI Limited 1994. All rights reserved.

Source: ONS and GRO(s) Crown Copyright 1991. All rights reserved.

96 and 1996-97). FRS results and FES results were compared. Table 5 summarises the analysis, showing that there was greater variation in FES response rates (47 to 75 per cent compared with the FRS range of 55 to 76 per cent) and in non-contact rates (zero per cent to 16 per cent compared with two to 11 per cent). In both cases the lowest response rate came from the 'Partially gentrified multi-ethnic areas'. The ACORN Type with the highest rate of response to the FES and FRS was the 'Agricultural villages, home based workers' group.

For the FES, the areas of higher response were characterised as family areas, having high proportions of skilled workers or home ownership, or as rural areas. These areas had both low non-contact and refusal rates - an exception being 'Multi-occupied terraces, multi-ethnic areas' which had a relatively high non-contact rate (five per cent) but was offset by a very low refusal rate (24 per cent). Areas of low response can be explained by either high refusal (for multi-ethnic areas and those with young professionals) or high non-contact (for areas with flats or single people) rates.

FRS non-response and Council Tax band

Comparisons were made between 1999-2000 FRS data and administrative data on the number of households within each Council Tax band. The analysis showed that FRS proportions were similar to those obtained from examining administrative data.

There were slight differences between countries (see Table 6). FRS data in England had a higher proportion of Band D households, but otherwise closely followed the pattern obtained from administrative data. Compared to administrative data, the FRS Scottish sample had a lower proportion of Band A households and a higher proportion of Band B households; Wales had a lower proportion of Band E households.

DSS, Family Resources Survey Great Britain 1999-2000, © Crown Copyright 2001

Table 6: Proportion of households in each Council Tax band by country: FRS data and administrative data

Council Tax band	England		Wales		Scotland	
	Administrative data	1999-00 FRS	Administrative data	1999-00 FRS	Administrative data	1999-00 FRS
Band A	26%	25%	20%	19%	26%	24%
Band B	19%	18%	25%	25%	25%	27%
Band C	21%	21%	20%	21%	15%	15%
Band D	15%	17%	15%	16%	12%	12%
Band E	9%	9%	12%	10%	11%	12%
Band F	5%	5%	4%	5%	6%	6%
Band G	3%	3%	3%	2%	4%	4%
Band H	1%	1%	-	-	-	-
Not valued separately	1%	1%	1%	2%	1%	1%
Total households (base=100%)	20,673,000	21,447	2,166,000	1,358	1,192,000	2,183

Non-response form analysis

Direct information about the non-responding households is valuable, although by definition difficult to obtain. However some households who are not willing to take part in the full survey may be willing to provide some basic information by completing a non-response form.

For the 1997-98 FRS interviewers carried out a short non-response form to collect information on households not taking part in the main survey. The non-response form tested asked about household relationships, age, working status, certain benefits, tenure and motor vehicles. Analysis of the data has been carried out and a report produced by the survey contractors. Highlights from the report are given below. It should be noted that only 33 per cent of households who declined to take part in the main survey agreed to provide some answers to the non-response form. Thus, results from the non-response form do not cover the majority of non-responders to the main FRS questionnaire and so should be treated with caution:

- 49 per cent of these households had no adult in paid work

- 21 per cent of these households had children, compared to 31 per cent of households who took part in the main survey

- nine per cent of these households had someone receiving Income Support, compared to 13 per cent of households who took part in the main survey

- 66 per cent of these households had access to a motor vehicle, compared to 70 per cent of households who took part in the main survey

Because of the low response to the non-response form, an experiment was carried out using four different non-response forms between August and November 1998. For all forms the response rate was high (73 per cent to 80 per cent). The response form varied in the number of questions asked and the topics covered. The results from the experiment were used to produce a new non-response form for the 1999-2000 survey year. Overall information about non-contacts was recorded in approximately 72% of cases.

Comparisons with other surveys

Some of the information collected by the FRS is also available in other Government surveys and comparisons of results can be a useful method of validation.

For example, FRS results have been compared with the Family Expenditure Survey (FES) in the context of Households Below Average Income (HBAI) analysis. Appendix 9 of the 1996/7 HBAI report details comparisons between the FRS and the FES. The main findings were that lower equivalised income was recorded in the FRS, particularly for singles and couples without children and also lower investment income, particularly for pensioners.

Analysis of 1997-98 FRS data suggests that estimates of the International Labour Organisation (ILO) definition of economic status compare favourably with estimates produced on an equivalent basis from the Labour Force Survey (LFS). Both sources showed that 59 per cent of adults were classified as employed, four per cent were classified as unemployed and 37 per cent as economically inactive. Figures are given to the nearest per cent.

Analysis of the LFS was carried out in such a way as to be as consistent with FRS data as possible. This was achieved by averaging LFS data over four quarters from March 1997 to February 1998 and only considering those individuals aged 16 or over (excluding those aged 16 to 18 who were in full time education) living in private households in Great Britain.

Validation, editing conversion and imputation

In addition to unit non-response, where a household does not participate, a problem inherent in all large surveys is item non-response. This occurs when a household agrees to give an interview, but either does not know the answer to certain questions or refuses to answer them (see the section on response in this chapter for further information). They are still classified as fully co-operating households because there is enough known data to be of good use to the analyst.

The fact that the FRS allows missing values in the data can create problems for users. It was therefore decided before the first full year's FRS data was released, that missing values should be imputed where appropriate. The policy has been that for variables which are components of key derived variables, such as gross household income and housing costs, and areas key to the work of the Department, such as benefit receipt, there should be no missing information in the final data.

In addition to imputation, prior to publication, FRS data must be put through several stages of validation and editing. This is to ensure that the final data presented to the public are as accurate as possible.

The stages in the validation, editing, conversion and imputation process are laid out below.

Stage one - the interview

As noted previously, one of the benefits of interviewing using CAPI is that in-built checks can be made at the interview stage. If answers are inconsistent or outside a certain range, the interviewer will receive a warning message instructing them to check that what the respondent is saying is correct. This method helps to check both respondents' responses and that interviewers do not make keying errors. There are checks to ensure that amounts are within a valid range and also cross-checks which make sure that an answer does not contradict a previous response. However, it is not possible to check all potential inconsistencies as this would slow down the program to an unacceptable degree, and there are also capacity constraints on text messages. Interviewers can override most checks if the answers are found to be accurate when confirmed with respondents.

Stage two - post-interview checks

Once an interview has taken place, data are returned to the Office for National Statistics or the National Centre for Social Research. Here a certain amount of editing takes place, mostly based on any notes made by interviewers. Notes are made by the interviewer when a warning has been overridden. These may be, for example, where an amount is outside the specified range, but the respondent has documentation to prove it is correct. Office-based staff make edit decisions based on these notes. Other edits that take place at this stage are checking amounts of fixed rate benefits such as Child Benefit and, where possible, separating multiple benefit payments into their constituent parts.

Stage three - data conversion

Before it can be validated further, FRS data must be converted from its CAPI format into SAS readable tables. Using DSS specifications SAS tables are created by the Office for National Statistics, each table recording different information from the questionnaire. Both the DSS and the Office for National Statistics then carry out validation checks on key input and output variables to ensure that the data have converted correctly to the new format. Checks include ensuring that the number of adults and children recorded is correct, and that records are internally consistent.

Stage four - pre-imputation cleaning

In preparation for imputing missing values, data are made as clean as possible. This involves edits and checks of the following nature:

Weekly amounts

In the FRS, all amounts received or paid are converted to a weekly value. To calculate this, respondents are usually asked firstly the amount last paid or received and then the length of time this covered. This is known as a period code. As part of the conversion process outlined in Stage three, period codes are used in conjunction with amount variables to give weekly totals for all receipts and payments. Some variables, such as interest on savings accounts, refer to the amount paid in the last year. These are also converted to a weekly amount.

Sometimes the period code relates to a lump sum or a one-off payment. In these cases the corresponding value does not automatically convert to a weekly amount. In order for the data to be consistent across the survey, edits are applied to convert lump sums and one-off payments to weekly amounts. In the same way, where period codes were previously recorded as 'don't know' or 'refused', these are imputed so that the corresponding amount can be converted to a weekly value in the final database.

Zero amounts

In previous years it was possible for interviewers to enter zero amounts when it is inappropriate to do so, for example in response to a question on receipt of benefit, when in fact the amount should be entered as missing. This created problems at later stages of analysis. From 1997-98, zero amounts can no longer be entered without a warning message to the interviewer. Some interviewers tried to avoid this message by recording near-zero amounts. These are also examined.

Outliers

Statistical reports of the data are produced to show individual cases where an amount was greater than five standard deviations away from the mean. For these cases the individual record is examined and where necessary (if a value looked unrealistic) the case is edited. The outliers remaining in the database are verified as being true values by examining other relevant data. Compared to earlier years, the number of these types of edits that now have to be carried out are small because of range checks that have been put into the CAPI questionnaire.

Credibility checks

Checks are carried out for the internal consistency of certain variables. For example it is ensured that there are no benefit units containing only one adult where the respondent states that they are married and their partner is in the household. Such cases are examined and edited where necessary.

Stage five - imputation

The responses to some questions are much more likely to have missing values than others. For example, it is very unlikely that a respondent will refuse to give, or will not know, their age or marital status, whereas it is much more likely that they will not be able to provide detailed information on the exact amounts of interest received from an investment.

The two areas where missing values are a major problem are income from self employment and income from investments.

Data in the tables provided in this publication include imputed values. However, for some variables missing values remain.

Table 7 illustrates the extent of the problem of missing values. It should be noted that out of over 11 million set values in the FRS database, only 0.5 per cent were originally recorded as either 'don't know' or 'refused'. Out of 57,419 missing values, approximately 93 per cent were imputed.

Table 7: Summary of imputation in 1998-1999 and 1999-2000 FRS

	1998-1999		1999-2000	
	Values	Percentage of values	Values	Percentage of values
Responses				
Expected number of responses	11,496,549	100	11,938,060	100
Valid responses	11,451,417	99.6	11,880,641	99.5
Missing values (don't know/refused)	45,132	0.4	57,419	0.5
Treatment of missing values				
Hotdeck	27,782	62	41,220	72
Bulk Edits	3,364	7	9,638	17
Other imputation method	8,124	18	582	1
Benefit editing	1,540	3	1,701	3
Left as Missing	4,322	10	4,278	7

A combination of methods of imputation were used for the 1999-2000 FRS data. The main ones are summarised below in the order in which they were used.

Closing down routes

As with any questionnaire, a typical feature of the FRS is the gatekeeper question positioned at the top of a block of further questions, at which a particular response will open up the block. If the gatekeeper question itself is answered as 'don't know' or 'refused', the block is skipped. This results in a potential problem.

A missing gatekeeper variable could be imputed such that a further series of answers would be expected. However, these answers will not appear because a whole new route has been opened. For example, if the amount of rent is missing for a record and has since been imputed, any further questions about rent would not have been asked. From the post-imputed database, it will appear that these questions should have been asked because a value is there for rent.

This is why, where appropriate, the decision was taken that with manual imputations a route should be closed down. In most cases, gatekeeper variables are of the 'yes/no' type. These would be imputed to 'no', assuming that if a respondent does not know whether an item is received or paid, then it is not.

Hotdecking

Hotdecking essentially looks at characteristics within a record containing the missing value to be imputed and matches it up to another record with similar characteristics

for which the variable is not missing. It then takes the known variable and copies it to the missing case. For example, for imputing the amount included in rent for services, classes of Council Tax band, number of bedrooms and Standard Statistical Region are used to search for a case with a similar record. This method ensures that imputed solutions are realistic, and gives a wide range of solutions maintaining variability in the data.

Algorithms

Algorithms are used to impute missing values for certain variables, for example variables relating to education grants and to Council Tax. The algorithms range from very simple calculations to more sophisticated models based on observed relationships within the data and individual characteristics such as age and sex.

'Mop-up' imputation

This is achieved by running a general validation report of all variables and looking at those cases where missing values were still present. At this stage, variables are looked at on a case-by-case basis to decide what to impute.

Credibility checks are then re-run to ensure that imputation had not resulted in any inconsistencies in the data, and edits were applied where necessary.

All imputations, by each of the methods above, are applied to the unimputed data set via a transaction database. This ensures that it is always possible to reproduce the original data.

DSS, Family Resources Survey Great Britain 1999-2000, © Crown Copyright 2001

Table 8: Extent of imputation

Variable	Actual number missing	Percentage of final values imputed	Method of Imputation
2nd loan repayment incl interest/capital	4	80	HOTDECK
1st loan repayment incl interest/capital	15	68	HOTDECK
Amount of National insurance lump sum	300	64	HOTDECK
Higher/lower rate of SMP	11	55	ALGORITHM
How much income tax deducted last time	114	42	HOTDECK
Amount included in rent for water/sewerage	762	40	ALGORITHM+HOTDECK
Amount of profit before tax	128	39	BULK EDIT
Amount included in last wage for SMP	20	31	ALGORITHM
Amount: Insurance part of repayment	1,022	29	ALGORITHM+HOTDECK
Whether investment interest before or after tax	86	28	BULK EDIT+HOTDECK
Whether net profit or loss before or after tax	661	28	BULK EDIT+HOTDECK
Amount from absent partner paid directly	15	28	HOTDECK
Whether making profit or loss	649	26	BULK EDIT+HOTDECK
Amount received from absent partner	9	26	HOTDECK
Amount of tax in last 12mths (self-employed)	416	26	HOTDECK
Amount of net profit or loss	648	25	HOTDECK
Maintenance via DSS - usual amount	1	25	HOTDECK

Table 8 lists the variables for 1999-2000 for which more than 25 per cent of final values were imputed.

Points to note with imputed data

Although a great deal of time has been spent on imputing missing values, it should be remembered that they represent only a very small proportion of the dataset as a whole. However, the following points should be noted:

- as mentioned above, in certain situations, imputed values will be followed by 'skipped' values. It was decided that it was better to impute the top of a route only and not to impute large amounts of data. There are a small proportion of imputations for which it was not appropriate to close down a route. These cases are followed by 'skipped' responses (where a value might otherwise be expected).

- imputation will have a greater effect in distorting the distribution of original data for variables that have a higher proportion of non-response, as proportions of imputed data will be higher.

Stage six - Benefit validation

Information on Social Security Benefits received is one of the key areas of the FRS and it is very important that this section is thoroughly validated and cleaned.

It is not appropriate to use the imputation methods outlined above for benefits data so instead a separate procedure of validation and editing is used. The following types of validation were carried out for 1999-2000 FRS data:

Missings

For cases where a respondent had answered 'yes' to whether they were in receipt of a particular benefit, but had not given the amount received, an imputation decision was made depending on the benefit. For benefits such as Income Support, where the rate would vary greatly depending on the situation of the respondent, individual benefit assessments were carried out. However, for benefits such as Retirement Pension, where fewer rates apply, a more general program could be written.

Near zero amounts

Where benefit amounts were recorded as near zero, the case was examined individually and an edit decision was made.

Multiple benefits

Any remaining combined benefit amounts (for example where Retirement Pension is paid with Income Support) not split at the office editing stage were edited by carrying out benefit entitlement assessments on individual cases, while preserving the reported total.

Attendance Allowance

It has been noted in previous years that the FRS under-reports receipt of Attendance Allowance (AA). In the past receipt of Retirement Pension (RP) was investigated to assess whether the amounts might include AA. If the amount of RP received was above a certain threshold, AA cases were created for these respondents. To deal with this, from 1997-98 extra questions were asked of RP recipients on whether the amount of RP they stated that they received included AA or Disability Living Allowance (Care component) or Disability Living Allowance (Mobility component). An assessment was then made on whether AA recipients were receiving higher rate or lower rate AA based on the amount they received for their RP.

Validation reports

Computer programs were run to carry out a final check for benefit entitlement and to output any cases that looked unreasonable. All cases detected as a result of this validation exercise were individually checked and edited where necessary.

Quality of benefits data

As part of the data validation process, comparisons are made between the FRS and other data sources. Table 9 shows a comparison of FRS benefit recipients compared to administrative data. The table shows both FRS sample data and grossed up sample estimates (see explanation of grossing factors in next section). Despite much time and effort being spent on benefit validation, there are still areas where there are known problems with the FRS data. The FRS under reports receipt for most of the benefits. The discrepancy between FRS and administrative data is particularly pronounced for Attendance Allowance, Severe Disability Allowance and Jobseeker's Allowance.

Users should note that some of the discrepancies in the two sources of data may be due to the fact that it is not always possible to compare like with like. Adjustments are made to try and eliminate some of the differences between the two sources. For example, the denominator for the administrative and the FRS data in Table 9 is the same and the administrative data figures for Retirement Pension and Widow's Benefit have been adjusted to remove those resident overseas. However, the fact that the FRS only interviews members of private households whereas administrative benefit systems (apart from Income Support) do not distinguish between people in private households and those in institutions remains a problem in comparing the two sources. For most benefits, only a very small minority of recipients will be in institutions, but this will have a greater effect on Attendance Allowance comparisons.

DSS, Family Resources Survey Great Britain 1999-2000, © Crown Copyright 2001

Table 9: Individuals in receipt of Social Security benefits

	1999-00 FRS		1999-00 FRS		DSS administrative data	Individuals
	Grossed		Sample			
Benefit received	Number	Percentage	Number	Percentage	Number	Percentage
Family Credit/Working Families' Tax Credit[1]	677,000	1.5	802	1.8	784,000	1.8
Income Support[2]	3,181,000	7.3	3,391	7.7	3,547,000	8.1
Housing Benefit[3]	4,244,000	9.7	4,585	10.4	4,243,000	9.7
Council Tax Benefit[3]	5,370,000	12.3	5,802	13.2	5,083,000	11.6
Jobseeker's Allowance[4]	971,000	2.2	843	1.9	1,097,000	2.5
Retirement Pension[5]	9,619,000	22.0	10,596	24.0	10,131,000	23.1
Widow's Benefit[6]	247,000	0.6	287	0.7	247,000	0.6
Incapacity Benefit[7]	1,492,000	3.4	1,479	3.4	1,538,000	3.5
Severe Disablement Benefit[8]	241,000	0.6	223	0.5	370,000	0.8
Attendance Allowance[9]	834,000	1.9	890	2.0	1,267,000	2.9
Invalid Care Allowance[9]	378,000	0.9	374	0.8	375,000	0.9
Disability Living Allowance (Care Component)[10]	1,205,000	2.8	1,199	2.7	1,483,000	3.4
Disability Living Allowance (Mobility Component)[10]	1,401,000	3.2	1,413	3.2	1,808,000	4.1
Child Benefit[11]	6,873,000	15.7	7,920	18.0	7,090,000	16.2
Total adults[12]	43,786,251	100.0	44,107	100.0	43,786,251	100.0

[1] Administrative data as at August 1999.

[2] Administrative data as at August 1999 – data adjusted to remove those in institutional accommodation for Income Support.

[3] MIS data August 1999 – data adjusted to remove those in institutional accommodation for Income Support.

[4] Administrative data at August 1999, excludes JSA Nil benefit cases.

[5] Administrative data at September 1999, figure excludes receeipients resident overseas.

[6] Widow's Pension and Widowed Mother's Allowance, figure excludes recipients resident overseas, administrative data as at September 1999.

[7] Administrative data as at 31 August 1999.

[8] Administrative data as at 31 August 1999.

[9] Administrative data as at 31 September 1999.

[10] Includes those receiving both care and mobility components, figure excludes recipients under 16, administrative data at 31 August 1999.

[11] Administrative data as at 30 August 1999.

[12] FRS figure used as a base for both comparisons and excludes those aged 16-18 in full time nonadvanced education.

Estimation methodology

The 1999-2000 FRS publication presents tabulations where the percentages refer to sample estimates grossed up to apply to the whole population.

Grossing up is the term usually given to the process of applying factors to sample data so that they yield estimates for the overall population. The simplest grossing system would be a single factor, the uniform grossing factor, which could be calculated as the number of households in the population divided by the number in the achieved sample. However, surveys are normally grossed by a more complex set of grossing factors, which attempt to correct for differential non-response at the same time as they scale up sample estimates.

The system used to calculate grossing factors for the FRS divides the sample into different groups and the grossing factors are the ratio of population estimates to sample counts for those groups. The groups are designed to reflect differences in response rates among different types of households. They have also been chosen with the aims of DSS analyses in mind. The population estimates are based on control variables, with values derived from external data sources.

The control variables and their sources are listed below. The FRS grossing system controls for variables at both household level and benefit unit level. A grossed count of the number of owner occupying households would thus tie in with the DETR figure, whilst the grossed number of single men under 35 would be consistent with the Office for National Statistics estimate. Some adjustments have been made to the original control total data sources so that definitions match those in the FRS. e.g. an adjustment has been made to the demographic data to exclude people not resident in private households.

In order to reconcile control variables at different levels and estimate their joint population, software provided by the French national statistics institute INSEE has been used. This software works by iterating towards a solution and options within it that give the solution which minimises the range of grossing factors have been used. This should maximise the potential precision of grossed estimates; if a few cases are associated with very small or very large grossing factors, grossed estimates will have relatively wide confidence intervals.

Careful consideration has been given to the combination of control totals and the way age ranges, Council Tax bands and so on, have been grouped together. The aim has been to strike a balance so that the grossing system will provide, where possible, accurate estimates in different dimensions without significantly increasing variances. Further details of how the FRS grossing system was developed are available in a DSS Analytical Note.

Reliability of estimates

All survey estimates have a sampling error attached to them, calculated from the variability of the observations in the sample. From this, a margin of error (confidence interval) is derived. It is this confidence interval (rather than the estimate itself) which is used to make statements about the likely 'true' value in the population; specifically, to state the probability that the true value will be found between the upper and lower limits of the confidence interval. In general, a confidence interval of twice the standard error is used to state, with 95 per cent confidence, that the true value falls within that interval. A small margin of error will result in a narrow interval, and hence a more precise estimate of where the true value lies.

The calculation of sampling errors (and thus confidence intervals) is based on an assumption of a simple random sampling method, but in practice this is almost never used with large general population surveys, due to its inefficiencies with regard to cost and time. The sample for the FRS, as described earlier, is selected using a stratified multi-stage design, based on addresses clustered into postal sectors. The sampling error estimate is therefore not simply based on the variability among all units in the sample (whether households or individuals) but must also take into account the variability within and between postal sectors. If a sample characteristic is distributed differently by postal sector (i.e. is clustered) this produces a greater overall variance than would occur in a simple random sample of the same size. In other words, the complex (actual) sampling error is greater than the (assumed) simple random sampling error.

Control variables used to generate grossing factors

Variable	Groupings	Source of data
Age/sex/marital status	Single men: <35, 35-59, 60+ Single women: <35, 35-64, 65+ Couples: <65, 65+	Office for National Statistics, Government Actuary's Department
Lone parents	Male, female	DSS estimates
Families	No. of couples with children	DSS estimates
Tenure type	LA renters, private renters, owner occupiers	DETR estimates
Council Tax Band	A, B, C-D, E-H	DETR estimates
Region	London, other	DETR estimates

The size of the actual standard error relative to the simple random sampling error is represented by the design factor (DEFT) which is calculated as the ratio of the two. Where the standard errors are the same, the DEFT is one, implying that there is no loss of precision associated with the use of a clustered sample design. In most cases, the DEFT will be greater than one, implying that the estimates based on the clustered sample are less precise than those for a simple random sample of the same size.

Tables 10 to 19 provide standard errors and design factors for a selection of variables from the 1999-2000 FRS. In common with other tabulations the percentages and sampling errors incorporate weighting factors which are designed to compensate for non-response. An example of how to interpret them follows:

Example: Table 10: Standard errors for household composition

Table 10 shows that 10.9 per cent of households were composed of one female adult over pension age. The standard error is 0.2. This can be interpreted in the following manner:

It can be estimated with 95 per cent confidence that the true percentage of households composed of one female adult over pension age is:

$10.9 \pm 2(0.2) = 10.9 \pm 0.4$

i.e. if sampling error is the sole source of error, the percentage of the population composed of one female adult over pension age is between 10.5 and 11.3 per cent, with 95 per cent confidence.

The design factor for this variable was 1.01. This implies that the effect of using a clustered sample rather than a simple random sample results in a loss of precision of one per cent on standard errors. Similarly, a design factor of 0.99 would have denoted a gain of precision of one per cent.

The sampling errors shown are likely to be slightly larger than the true sampling errors because the software used for the calculation does not take into account the improvement in precision due to post stratification.

In addition to sampling errors consideration should also be given to non-sampling errors. As is clear from the above discussion, the sampling errors generally arise through the process of random sampling and the influence of chance. Non-sampling errors arise from the introduction of some systematic bias in the sample as compared to the population it is supposed to represent. Besides response biases, considered above, there are several potential sources of such bias such as inappropriate definition of the population, misleading questions, data input errors or data handling problems - in fact any factor that might lead to the survey results systematically misrepresenting the population. There is no simple control or measurement for such non-sampling errors although the risk can be minimised through careful application of the appropriate survey techniques from questionnaire and sample design through to analysis of results.

Table 10: Standard errors for household composition

Household composition	Percentage of all households	Standard error	Design factor
Households without children			
One male adult			
over pension age	**3.4**	0.11	0.96
under pension age	**9.6**	0.22	1.18
One female adult			
over pension age	**10.9**	0.20	1.01
under pension age	**4.8**	0.14	1.04
Two adults			
both over pension age	**9.4**	0.18	0.97
one over pension age	**4.9**	0.15	1.10
both under pension age	**18.6**	0.26	1.06
Three or more adults	**9.2**	0.22	1.20
Households with children			
One adult			
one child	**2.6**	0.09	0.89
two children	**2.1**	0.08	0.88
three children or more	**1.2**	0.07	1.02
Two adults			
one child	**6.7**	0.16	1.01
two children	**8.4**	0.17	0.97
three children or more	**3.8**	0.12	0.99
Three or more adults			
one child	**2.7**	0.11	1.07
two children	**1.1**	0.07	1.06
three children or more	**0.5**	0.05	1.12
Total households without children	**70.9**	0.31	1.08
Total households with children	**29.1**	0.31	1.08
Total households	**24,988**		

Table 11: Standard errors for Council Tax band

Council Tax band	Percentage of all households	Standard error	Design factor
Band A	**25.9**	0.40	1.44
Band B	**20.0**	0.33	1.30
Band C	**19.3**	0.32	1.28
Band D	**15.6**	0.28	1.22
Band E	**9.1**	0.22	1.21
Band F	**4.7**	0.16	1.20
Band G	**3.4**	0.14	1.22
Band H	**0.5**	0.06	1.34
Not valued separately	**1.4**	0.11	1.48
Total households	**24,988**		

DSS, Family Resources Survey Great Britain 1999-2000, © Crown Copyright 2001

Table 12: Standard errors for gross weekly household income

Gross weekly household income	Percentage of all households	Standard error	Design factor
Wages and salaries	58.1	0.34	1.09
Self employment income	10.5	0.22	1.13
Investments	68.8	0.41	1.40
State Retirement Pension plus any IS	30.1	0.30	1.03
Other pensions	26.1	0.31	1.12
Social Security disability benefits	15.7	0.24	1.04
Other Social Security benefits	48.1	0.35	1.11
Other sources	15.3	0.26	1.14
Total households	**24,988**		

Table 13: Standard errors for sources of income

Source of income	Percentage of average gross weekly household income	Standard error	Design factor
All sources of income	100.0	-	.
Wages and salaries	64.1	0.40	1.14
Self employment income	9.1	0.36	1.04
Investments	3.0	0.09	1.14
State Retirement Pension plus any IS	6.1	0.09	1.12
Other pensions	6.7	0.14	1.12
Social Security disability benefits	2.5	0.05	1.23
Other Social Security benefits	6.3	0.10	1.36
Other sources	2.1	0.09	1.48
Total households	**24,988**		

Table 14: Standard errors for benefit receipt

Benefit units by benefit receipt	Percentage of all benefit units	Standard error	Design factor
Family Credit/Working Families' Tax Credit	2.3	0.09	1.03
Income Support	10.7	0.19	1.06
Housing Benefit	14.3	0.24	1.18
Council Tax Benefit	18.1	0.26	1.16
Retirement Pension	24.4	0.28	1.12
Widow's Benefit	1.0	0.05	0.86
Jobseeker's Allowance	3.2	0.12	1.17
Incapacity Benefit	4.8	0.13	1.05
Severe Disablement Allowance	0.8	0.06	1.16
Attendance Allowance	2.7	0.10	1.06
Invalid Care Allowance	1.3	0.07	1.06
Disability Living Allowance (care component)	4.4	0.13	1.09
Disability Living Allowance (mobility component)	4.8	0.13	1.05
Industrial Injuries Disablement Benefit	0.8	0.05	0.97
War Disablement Pension	0.6	0.04	0.89
Child Benefit	23.1	0.27	1.10
On any income related benefit	23.2	0.29	1.18
On any non-income related benefit	54.6	0.36	1.24
On any benefit	59.3	0.36	1.26
No benefits	40.7	0.36	1.26
Total benefit units	**29,575**		

DSS, Family Resources Survey Great Britain 1999-2000, © Crown Copyright 2001

Table 15: Standard errors for tenure and accommodation type

Tenure and type of accommodation	Percentage of all households	Standard error	Design factor
Rented accommodation			
Rented from:			
Council	**17.0**	0.33	1.39
Housing Association	**5.4**	0.20	1.40
All social sector rented tenants	**22.4**	0.36	1.36
Rented privately			
Unfurnished	**5.4**	0.18	1.26
Furnished	**4.7**	0.19	1.42
All rented privately	**10.1**	0.27	1.42
Accommodation			
House or bungalow			
Detached	**1.4**	0.09	1.21
Semi-detached	**7.4**	0.21	1.27
Terraced	**9.7**	0.23	1.23
All houses and bungalows	**18.5**	0.31	1.26
Flat or maisonette			
Purpose built	**11.0**	0.28	1.41
Non-purpose built	**2.4**	0.15	1.55
All flats or maisonettes	**13.4**	0.32	1.48
Other accommodation	**0.7**	0.08	1.52
Owner occupiers			
Tenure			
Buying with mortgage	**40.1**	0.38	1.23
Owned outright	**27.4**	0.34	1.21
All owners	**67.5**	0.41	1.38
Accommodation			
House or bungalow			
Detached	**19.3**	0.36	1.44
Semi-detached	**23.3**	0.38	1.42
Terraced	**19.0**	0.37	1.49
All houses and bungalows	**61.6**	0.45	1.46
Flat or maisonette			
Purpose built	**4.1**	0.16	1.28
Non-purpose built	**1.4**	0.10	1.35
All flats or maisonettes	**5.5**	0.19	1.32
Other accommodation	**0.4**	0.05	1.25
Total households	**24,988**		

Table 16: Standard errors for weekly housing costs

Weekly housing costs	Percentage of all households	Standard error	Design factor
Under £20 a week	31.9	0.36	1.22
£20 but under £40 a week	16.2	0.28	1.20
£40 but under £60 a week	23.9	0.33	1.22
£60 but under £80 a week	13.1	0.24	1.12
£80 but under £100 a week	6.4	0.17	1.10
£100 but under £150 a week	5.5	0.16	1.11
£150 a week or more	3.0	0.13	1.20
Total households	**24,988**		

Table 17: Standard errors for types of account held

Type of account	Percentage of all adults	Standard error	Design factor
Current account	83.0	0.27	1.51
Post Office account	5.3	0.14	1.31
TESSA	11.2	0.21	1.40
ISA	8.1	0.20	1.54
Other bank/building society	53.0	0.41	1.73
Gilts	0.7	0.05	1.26
Unit trusts	4.0	0.12	1.29
Stocks and shares	19.8	0.27	1.42
National Savings Bonds	3.5	0.11	1.26
Save As You Earn	1.0	0.06	1.27
Premium Bonds	18.7	0.28	1.51
PEPs	10.5	0.20	1.37
Any type of account	90.1	0.22	1.55
No accounts	9.9	0.22	1.55
ACT Compatible Account	89.6	0.23	1.58
Total adults	**44,107**		

DSS, Family Resources Survey Great Britain 1999-2000, © Crown Copyright 2001

Table 18: Standard errors for employment status

Adults by employment status	Percentage of all adults	Standard error	Design factor
Employee			
full time	39.9	0.28	1.20
part time	11.7	0.16	1.05
Self employed			
full time	5.4	0.12	1.12
part time	1.7	0.07	1.14
All in employment			
full time	45.3	0.28	1.18
part time	13.4	0.18	1.11
ILO unemployed	3.5	0.11	1.26
Retired	20.5	0.24	1.25
Student	1.6	0.12	2.01
Looking after family home	5.3	0.12	1.12
Permanently sick or disabled	6.3	0.14	1.21
Temporarily sick or disabled	0.4	0.03	1.00
Other inactive	3.8	0.11	1.21
Total adults	**44,107**		

Table 19: Standard errors for ethnic group of adults

Ethnic group	Percentage of all adults	Standard error	Design factor
White	94.1	0.31	2.76
Black	1.6	0.11	1.84
Indian	1.4	0.14	2.50
Pakistani/Bangladeshi	1.5	0.18	3.11
Other	1.5	0.10	1.73
Total adults	**44,107**		

GSS Harmonisation Project

In 1995, a number of Government Departments came together to discuss the best way of making the results of major official surveys comparable. This led to the Harmonisation Project, whereby the inputs – the questions and related interviewer instructions and edit checks - used in the major surveys, and outputs – the concepts for analysis and publication - from them, is identical in as many of the surveys as possible. A list of the current harmonised questions may be found at http://www.statistics.gov.uk/harmony/harmonfp.asp.

Different surveys have different purposes and hence cover topics in different depths. Harmonised questions are designed to provide the recommended minimum information to allow common classifications and facilitate the analysis of data from different surveys in combination. Not all surveys will include questions on all topics or in every year, but the recommendation is that, where a topic is covered, harmonised questions should be included wherever possible.

Some surveys will require further detail on topics than can be obtained from the harmonised questions alone. It will normally be the case that such surveys already ask for that detail. The harmonised questions have been designed so that the surveys which ask for more detail can either derive them, without asking them directly, or combine them with the further detail, without adding to the length of interview.

The FRS has actually set the standard for a number of harmonised questions, but many more on the FRS are being changed to fall in line with Government surveys such as the Survey of English Housing, the Family Expenditure Survey and the Labour Force Survey.

The table below summarises the status of harmonised outputs in this and previous FRS reports.

Topic	Outputs	Inputs (questions)
Accommodation type	1995-96	1996-97
Age last birthday	1997-98	Already harmonised, although full household grid only introduced in 1996-97; date of birth for those under 20 years from 1996-97.
Consumer Durables	N/A	1997-98. However, these are rotated off the FRS biannually. Therefore revised harmonised questions will not be implemented until 2001-02.
Economic Activity (ILO)	1996-97	1996-97
Ethnic origin	1994-95	1996-97
Gender	Already harmonised.	Already harmonised.
Geography - use of GORs	1995-96, although North West and Merseyside combined since 1996-97.	
Health	No tables use this classification, see Table 19 for further information.	1996-97
Household income	1996-97	Detailed questions harmonised with FES from 1996-97.
Household Reference Person	N/A	Piloted in 1999-2000, but will not affect outputs until 2001-02 as the likely impact of the change will have to be quantified.
Household response unit	Already harmonised.	Already harmonised.
Housing costs and benefits (Council Tax, Rent, Housing Benefit and Mortgages)	Output bands harmonised 1995-96 for rents. Differences in method of calculation of mortgage interest.	1997-98, also includes additional questions.

Topic	Outputs	Inputs (questions)
Industry, occupation, socio-economic classifications	Already harmonised.	Already harmonised. In questions on job description, present tense used for those currently in work.
Legal marital status	No tables use this breakdown.	1996-97
Length of residence	1996-97	1996-97 (original proposal) revised 1996-97 to include 20 year or more cut off.
Length of time since last in paid work	1996-97	1996-97
Living arrangements	1994-95	1997-98
Reference period	Already harmonised.	
Social Security benefits	More detailed breakdown used. Jobseeker's Allowance (contributions based) included with non-means tested benefits category. Definition of disability benefits is different from harmonised classification, which includes Invalid Care Allowance (ICA). ICA is paid to the carer not the severely disabled person being cared for.	Already harmonised.
Tenure	1994-95 (although minor differences in treatment of cases where accommodation goes with the job of someone in the household).	1996-97
Time in present job	No tables use this classification.	1996-97
Usual hours in main job	1996-97	1996-97
Vehicle ownership/continuous use	No tables use this classification, although tables showing consumer durables include light vans in the car category.	1996-97

Harmonised output categories for marital status, ethnic group, Social Security benefits, tenure, accommodation type, housing cost bands and length of residency have been included in previous publications although in some cases these were based on non-harmonised questions. From 1997-98 many more harmonised questions were included in the survey particularly in the area of housing costs and living arrangements.

Another area where the FRS output categories differ from harmonisation proposals is disability. The harmonised question for dealing with the health of individuals is:

Do you have any long-standing illness, disability or infirmity? By long-standing I mean anything that has troubled you over a period of time or that is likely to affect you over a period of time?

On the FRS, individuals who answer 'yes' to this question are also asked if this illness or disability limits their activities in any way and if they are registered disabled. In addition all adults below pension age are asked if they are restricted in the work they can do by some illness, injury or disability. Responses to all these questions are used to define sick or disabled adults for use in the household composition and economic status classifications (ILO definitions are based on those who have stated they cannot work or look for work because of sickness/disability). Table 20 shows health status by age group using the different definitions. As can be seen, the additional query about whether activities are limited by the illness or disability does affect the classification. The final column shows also that up to state retirement age there are some individuals who consider themselves restricted in the work they can do but have not categorised themselves as disabled.

Table 20: Long Standing Limiting Illness

Age group	Percentage of all adults		
	Long Standing Illness	Long Standing Limiting Illness	Long Standing Limiting Illness or Restricted in Work
16 to 24	13	8	8
25 to 34	15	10	10
35 to 44	20	13	13
45 to 54	29	19	20
55 to 59	38	27	28
60 to 64	46	33	34
65 to 74	53	36	37
75 to 84	63	49	49
85 or over	72	65	65
All adults	**31**	**22**	**22**
Total adults	**44,107**	**44,107**	**44,107**

Differences due to survey design features

Despite the use of harmonised inputs, there will inevitably be differences in the outputs of the varied surveys as a result of differences between the design of the surveys (and due to sampling variability). Primary among these is sample size; where the direct results of a survey are grossed up to estimate a total population, assumptions have to be made of the relevance of identified features to that population and it is reasonable to expect a wider margin of error from a sample of, say, 5,000 than from one of 50,000.

Relevant survey design features include:

- question wording and context effects;
- definition differences;
- non-response bias;
- geographical coverage;
- sampled population;
- mode effect;
- acceptance of proxy information;
- treatment of multi-households;
- unit of analysis;
- field practices;
- item non-response;
- time period;
- organisational effect.

Further details are provided in Amanda White and Sarah McCreith's 'An initial look at harmonised survey data', Survey Methodology Bulletin 43 (July 1998).

The GSS is continuing to try to quantify these likely differences, and advise users of official statistics of where such differences are likely to arise, the reasons for them, and the potential size of any.

Glossary/Notes on definitions

Adult

All those aged 16 and over, except for 16 to 18 year olds in full time non-advanced education; all adults in the *household* are interviewed as part of the FRS.

Age

Age last birthday (ie at time of interview).

Any benefit

Any Social Security benefit; tables in Chapter 3 show percentage of *benefit units/households* who received at least one Social Security benefit, *income related benefit* and *non-income related benefit*.

Includes receipt of benefits such as Disability Working Allowance, Disabled Person's Tax Credit, Back to Work Bonus and Maternity Benefits which are not shown separately in the tables.

Any type of account

Any account or investment for which information is collected on the survey. See also other entries for categories used in tables, ie *Current account, Post Office account, TESSA, Other bank/building society accounts, etc.*

Attendance Allowance

Social Security benefit for people aged 65 or over who need help with personal care because of a mental or physical disability. There are two rates, a lower rate for attendance during day or night, and a higher rate for day and night.

For more information see Social Security Statistics, (CDS, ISBN 1 84123 145 2).

Benefit unit

A single *adult* or couple living as married and any *dependent* children.

Child

All those aged under 16 or an unmarried 16 to 18 year old in full time non-advanced education.

Child Benefit

Social Security benefit paid for each child under 16 year or aged under 19 and still in full time non-advanced education. Usually received by the mother.

For more information see Social Security Statistics, (CDS, ISBN 1 84123 145 2).

Co-ownership schemes

Like *shared ownership* schemes. Usually where the landlord is a housing association.

Council Tax

Council Tax replaced the Community Charge from April 1993. The tax is based on the property value of a dwelling (which is split in to *bands*) and assumes two adults per household. The full bill consists of a property and a personal element.

Status discounts, which reduce or eliminate the personal element of the tax, are available to single person and certain other households.

An exemption may apply to some households, the most common type being accommodation occupied solely by students or where the accommodation is owned by the Ministry of Defence as armed forces' accommodation.

Council Tax band

Bands of property value of a dwelling as used in the calculation of *Council Tax*. Different bands exist in England, Scotland and Wales (valuation as at 1 April 1991):

	England	Scotland	Wales
Band A	up to £40,000	up to £27,000	up to £30,000
Band B	£40-52,000	£27-35,000	£30-39,000
Band C	£52-68,000	£35-45,000	£39-51,000
Band D	£68-88,000	£45-58,000	£51-66,000
Band E	£88-120,000	£58-80,000	£66-90,000
Band F	£120-160,000	£80-106,000	£90-120,000
Band G	£160-320,000	£106-212,000	£120-240,000
Band H	£320,000+	£212,000+	£240,000+

Council Tax band: not valued separately

Households where the landlord is liable for the tax, for example where they are sub-let as part of larger premises. The landlord may decide to recover some or all of the cost of the tax by increasing rent charges.

Council Tax Benefit

Social Security benefit administered by the local authority designed to help people on low incomes pay their Council Tax. There are two types of Council Tax Benefit, maximum Council Tax Benefit (Main Benefit) and Second Adult Rebate.

Council Tax Benefit may be received for a further 4 weeks by people aged under 60 when they start working full time following a period of at least 6 months being unemployed, on a Government Training Scheme or on *Income Support* as a lone parent or carer (Extended Payment).

For more information see Social Security Statistics, (CDS, ISBN 1 84123 145 2).

For tables in Chapter 3 which show *benefit units* by benefit receipt, Council Tax Benefit is allocated to the first *benefit unit* in the *household*.

Current account

Includes all current accounts with banks and building societies. Used for day to day transactions with a cheque book and/or bank card. Interest will normally be minimal.

Dependant

See *child*.

Disability Living Allowance

Social Security benefit for people who become disabled before the age of 65 and need help with personal care, getting around, or both. Consists of two components:

Care component

Covers personal care (eg washing, dressing, using the toilet, cooking a main meal). This is paid at three rates.

Mobility component

For those who cannot walk or have difficulty in walking. This is paid at two rates.

For more information see Social Security Statistics, (CDS, ISBN 1 84123 145 2).

DSS, Family Resources Survey Great Britain 1999-2000, © Crown Copyright 2001

Economic status

This classification is consistent with that used in *HBAI*. *Benefit units* are allocated to the first category which applies. Unlike *employment status,* full time work is classified as 31 hours or more, not on the basis of the respondent's assessment of whether they work full or part time.

Self employed

Benefit units (single and couple) where at least one *adult* usually works as self employed 31 hours or more a week.

Single or couple, all in full time work

Benefit units (single and couple) where all *adults* usually work 31 hours or more a week.

Couple, one in full time work, one in part time work

Benefit units headed by a couple, where one partner usually works 31 hours or more a week and the other partner usually works fewer than 31 hours a week.

Couple, one in full time work, one not working

Benefit units headed by a couple, where one partner usually works 31 hours or more a week and the other partner does not work.

One or more in part time work

Benefit units (singles and couples) where at least one *adult* works fewer than 31 hours a week.

Head or spouse aged 60 or over

Benefit units (singles and couples) where at least one *adult* is aged 60 or over.

Head or spouse unemployed

Benefit units (singles and couples) where at least one *adult* is *unemployed*. Also includes an additional check on receipt of *Jobseeker's Allowance*. If these are in receipt, the case is treated as unemployed even if did some unpaid work in business that they or relative owns. These respondents are treated as economically active in the *employment status* classification.

Head or spouse sick or disabled

Benefit units (singles and couples) where at least one *adult* is *sick or disabled*.

Others

Benefit units not classified above.

The full derivation of this variable is available on request from ASD3E, at the address listed in the Introduction.

Economically inactive

Those who are out of work but do not meet the criteria for *ILO unemployment* are economically inactive.

Employment status

This classification is equivalent to the harmonised output category for economic status (relabelled to avoid confusion with benefit unit level outputs – see Chapter 8 for more information on harmonisation). It is based on respondents' answers to questions on current employment status, notes below highlight main differences between this and *Economic status* and *Household Composition*.

The full derivation of this variable is available on request from ASD3E, at the address listed in the Introduction.

In Chapter 6, the category for other inactive also includes those classified as students, looking after family/ home and temporary sick and disabled adults.

Employee - full time

Based on self assessment for the main job rather than number of hours worked. Includes those doing unpaid work in a business that a relative owns.

Employee - part time

Based on self assessment for the main job rather than number of hours worked. Includes those doing unpaid work in a business that a relative owns.

Self employed - full time

Based on self assessment for the main job rather than number of hours worked. Includes those doing unpaid work in their own business.

Self employed - part time

Based on self assessment for the main job rather than number of hours worked. Includes those doing unpaid work in their own business.

Retired

Individuals who are over the age of 70 or say they are retired.

Endowment mortgage

An endowment policy is taken out with an insurance company either before or at the same time as the mortgage. When the policy matures the sum received will be used to repay the original sum borrowed under that mortgage.

The original mortgage amount remains outstanding until the policy matures, in the meantime the borrower pays interest to the lender and premiums on the endowment policy to the insurance company.

Endowment policy premiums are not included as part of *Housing Costs*.

Ethnic group

The group to which respondents consider they belong. The FRS (harmonised) question has 9 categories. The Black category consists of those responding as 'Black-Caribbean', 'Black-African' and 'Black-neither Caribbean or African'. The Other category consists of 'Chinese' and 'none of these'. For more information on harmonisation see Chapter 8.

Family Credit

Social Security benefit for working people who are responsible for at least one *child*. The claimant, or partner, must be working at least 16 hours per week (employed or self employed). This benefit has been phased out since October 1999 and replaced with the new Working Families' Tax Credit.

For more information see Social Security Statistics, (CDS, ISBN 1 84123 145 2).

Family status

This classification is based on the family type classification used in *HBAI* except that pensioner *households* are classified on the basis of the head of the *benefit unit*, regardless of the sex (for *HBAI*, the head is always male).

Tables also include *benefit units* where the partner is temporarily not in the *household* (eg where they are working abroad) which are excluded from *HBAI* analyses.

The full derivation of this variable is available on request from ASD3E, at the address listed in the Introduction.

Pensioner couple

Benefit units headed by a couple, where the head of the *benefit unit* is over *state pension age*.

Single male pensioner

Benefit units headed by a single male *adult* over *state pension age*.

Single female pensioner

Benefit units headed by a single female *adult* over *state pension age*.

Couple with children

Benefit units headed by a (non-pensioner) couple with *dependent* children.

Couple without children

Benefit units headed by a (non-pensioner) couple with no *dependent* children.

Single with children

Benefit units headed by a (non-pensioner) single *adult* with *dependent* children.

Single male without children

Benefit units headed by a (non-pensioner) single male *adult* with no *dependent* children.

Single female without children

Benefit units headed by a (non-pensioner) single female *adult* with no *dependent* children.

Full time education

Individuals registered as full time at an educational establishment. Students on sandwich courses are coded as students or working according to their position at the time of interview.

Gilts

Government Gilt-edged stock (including War Loan). 'Gilts' raise money for the UK Government by offering a secure investment, usually over a fixed period and with a fixed rate of interest, although some are index-linked. Interest is paid half-yearly.

Gilts can be bought and sold. At the end of the fixed term the holder is repaid the original purchase price. The value of the gilt is the current market price.

Gross weekly benefit unit income

Weekly income from all sources for all *adults* and *children* in the *benefit unit*.

The full derivation of this variable is available on request from ASD3E, at the address listed in the Introduction.

Gross weekly household income

Weekly income from all sources for all *adults* and *children* in the *household*.

The full derivation of this variable is available on request from ASD3E, at the address listed in the Introduction.

HBAI

Households Below Average Income, A Statistical Analysis 1994/5 - 1998/9 (CDS).

Head of benefit unit

The *head of the benefit unit* will either be the same as the *head of the household* if it is the benefit unit to which the head of the household belongs, or if not, it will be the first person in the benefit unit. For all *benefit units* in the *household* which are couples, the head will usually be the male, but in certain circumstances may be female.

Head of household

The *head of the household* will be the *head of the benefit unit* which he or she belongs to.

Interviewers classify the head of household using standard procedures:

In a household containing only husband, wife and children under 16 (and boarders) the husband is always the head of household.

Similarly, when a couple have been recorded as living together/cohabiting the male partner is treated as the head of household.

In all situations where there are other relatives in the household or where some or all of the household are unrelated, except that a husband always takes precedence, the person in whose name the accommodation is owned or rented is taken as the head.

When the accommodation is supplied with a job or provided rent free for some other reason, the person to whom the accommodation is given in this way becomes the head.

Occasionally more than one person will have equal claim to be the head, in these cases, where they are of the same sex, the oldest is the head; where they are of different sexes, the male is the head.

Household

A single person or group of people living at the same address as their only or main residence, who either share one meal a day together or share the living accommodation (ie living room). A household will consist of one or more *benefit units.*

Household composition

The classification of households into those with and without *children* leads to mutually exclusive categories, which add to the total number of households in the sample. The other categories shown may overlap.

The full derivation of this variable is available on request from ASD3E, at the address listed in the Introduction.

Households with one or more adults over pension age

Households where at least one *adult* is over *state pension age.*

Households with one or more sick or disabled adults under pension age

Households where at least one *adult* is classified as *sick or disabled.*

Households with one or more unemployed adults

Households where at least one *adult* is *unemployed,* as defined by the International Labour Organisation (ILO).

Household rent

Actual rent paid by the household,

plus any *Housing Benefit,*

plus contributions made by someone outside the household,

less water and sewerage charges included in rent (including Council Tax Water Charge in Scotland) and other services ineligible for *Housing Benefit* purposes. The latter includes payments for lighting, heating, hot water, fuel, food, TV rental etc.

Amounts are adjusted for rent holidays where appropriate.

The full derivation of this variable is available on request from ASD3E, at the address listed in the Introduction.

Housing Benefit

Social Security benefit administered by local authorities which is designed to help people who rent their homes and have difficulty meeting their housing costs.

Council tenants on Housing Benefit get a rent rebate which means that their rent due is reduced by the amount of that rebate.

Private and housing association tenants usually receive Housing Benefit (or rent allowance) personally, although sometimes it is paid direct to the landlord.

DSS, Family Resources Survey Great Britain 1999-2000, © Crown Copyright 2001

Housing Benefit may be received for a further 4 weeks by people aged under 60 when they start working full time following a period of at least 6 months being unemployed, on a Government Training Scheme or on *Income Support* as a lone parent or carer (Extended Payment).

For more information see Social Security Statistics, (CDS, ISBN 1 84123 145 2).

Housing costs

Household rent for rented accommodation or *mortgage interest* for those buying their home with a mortgage, **plus** water and sewerage charges (including Council Tax Water Charge in Scotland),

plus premiums paid on structural insurance

plus charges for owner occupiers (ground rent, fuel duties, service charges etc.),

The full derivation of this variable is available on request from ASD3E, at the address listed in the Introduction.

ILO Unemployed

Adults who are under *state pension age* and not working but are available and have been actively seeking work in the last four weeks. Includes those who were waiting to take up a job already obtained and will start in the next two weeks.

Income related benefits

Social Security benefits included in this category are:

Back To Work Bonus

Extended Payment of *Council Tax Benefit*

Extended Payment of *Housing Benefit*

Income Support

Family Credit/Working Families' Tax Credit

Housing Benefit

Council Tax Benefit

Disability Working Allowance/Disabled Person's Tax Credit

Social Fund Grant for Funeral Expenses

Social Fund Grant for Maternity Expenses

Jobseeker's Allowance (Income based)

Community Care Grants

Incapacity Benefit

Replaced Sickness Benefit and Invalidity Benefit from 13 April 1995. It is paid to people who are assessed as being incapable of work and who meet the contribution conditions.

For more information see Social Security Statistics, (CDS, ISBN 1 84123 145 2).

Income Support

Social Security benefit for adults aged 18 or over who are working less than 16 hours a week and who have less money coming in than the law says they need to live on. In general, IS is now only available to people who are not required to be available for work such as pensioners, lone parents and sick and disabled people.

It is made up of personal allowances for each member of the *benefit unit*, premiums for any special needs and housing costs, principally for mortgage interest payments.

Often paid to top up other benefits or earnings from part time work.

For more information see Social Security Statistics, (CDS, ISBN 1 84123 145 2).

Informal carers

Adults or *children* who provide any regular service or help to someone in or outside their *household* who is sick, disabled or elderly. Excludes those who give this help as part of a formal job.

Industrial Injuries Disablement Benefit

Social Security benefit provided for employees who are disabled because of an industrial accident or prescribed industrial disease. To get the basic benefit the person needs a medical assessment of the degree of their disability.

For more information see Social Security Statistics, (CDS, ISBN 1 84123 145 2).

Insurance cover

The FRS asks about insurance policies to find out what types of personal cover members of the *household* have. Personal accident includes: personal accident and fire, personal accident policy for a pedal cycle, personal consolidation policy, police group insurance. Private medical includes BUPA, HCS, and PPA WPA. Permanent health insurance or PHI is insurance to cover loss of income in the event of permanent health impairment. Friendly society policies for sickness include Benevolent fund, Burial club, Post Office and Civil Service Sanatorium Society, Death levy, Family Service Unit, Firemen's benevolent fund, Hospital Savings Association, Hospital Saturday Fund, Medical aid, Mutual aid, Oddfellows.

Invalid Care Allowance

Social Security benefit for people who are eligible before their 65th birthday, who are not employed or in full time education and who look after a severely disabled person for at least 35 hours per week.

The severely disabled person must be getting either higher or middle rate *Disability Living Allowance Care component* or *Attendance Allowance* or a Constant Attendance Allowance at the maximum rate under the War Pensions or Industrial Injuries Scheme.

For more information see Social Security Statistics, (CDS, ISBN 1 84123 145 2).

ISA

Individual Savings Account. It is a Government tax free savings scheme which replaced PEP and TESSA in April 1999. It is usually arranged via a bank or building society.

Jobseeker's Allowance

Replaced Unemployment Benefit and *Income Support* for unemployed people on 7 October 1996. It is payable to people under *state pension age* who are available for, and actively seeking, work of at least 40 hours per week. Certain groups of people, including carers and those with a physical or mental condition, are able to restrict their availability to less than 40 hours depending upon their personal circumstances.

There are contribution based and income based routes of entry to Jobseeker's Allowance. The different elements are separated in the any *income related benefit* and any *non-income related benefit* categories. However, the individual row for Jobseeker's Allowance shown in Chapter 3 tables includes both elements.

For more information see Social Security Statistics, (CDS, ISBN 1 8412 3 145 2).

Main source of weekly income

This is the source of income which has the highest figure when expressed as a percentage of total weekly income. Figures should be interpreted with caution: for example a *household* might in fact have similar proportions of income from two or more sources.

Marital status

As recorded by the respondent. Single means never married. Single sex couples are classified as single since for benefit purposes they count as two separate *benefit units*.

DSS, Family Resources Survey Great Britain 1999-2000, © Crown Copyright 2001

Mortgage interest

For *endowment, pension, PEP and Unit Trust* mortgages quoted mortgage interest figures are used. For *repayment mortgages,* interest is calculated on the basis of amount of mortgage outstanding multiplied by the interest rate current at the time of interview.

Quoted interest figures are checked to ensure that other payments (eg for mortgage protection policies, structural insurance or interest on top-up loans for purposes unrelated to housing costs) are excluded and adjusted to include payments made by individuals outside the *household*. Figures are also net of tax relief.

The full derivation of this variable is available on request from ASD3E, at the address listed in the Introduction.

National Savings Bonds

Tables include all types of National Savings investments in this category collected on the survey:

FIRST Option Bonds

Accumulating lump sum investment of between £1,000 and £250,000. Interest is paid net of tax and credited annually. The rate is reviewed each year and holders have the option to withdraw or continue.

National Savings Capital Bonds

Minimum purchase £100, maximum holding £250,000. Interest fixed for 5 years and credited annually gross of tax (although taxable).

National Savings Certificates

Fixed and index-linked to changes in the RPI. For lump sum savings of £100 or more. Maximum earnings are obtained after 5 years. Interest on both investments is tax free.

Pensioner's Guaranteed Income Bonds.

Available to people over 65. Gives a fixed interest rate over 5 years with income paid monthly gross of tax. Minimum investment £500.

National Savings Income Bonds

Minimum purchase £2,000, maximum £250,000. Interest is paid monthly gross of tax (although taxable).

National Savings Deposit Bonds

Multiples of £50, offering premium rates of interest gross of tax. No longer available, but earlier bonds are still valid.

Children's Bonus Bonds

Can be bought for any child under 16. A 5 year accumulating investment. Interest is paid gross of tax.

Yearly Plan

Yearly plan certificates can still be held, though new applications stopped in January 1995. Under the scheme monthly standing order payments of £20 were made (to a maximum of £400); after 12 months a Yearly Plan certificate was issued. The certificates earn tax free interest, paid monthly, and reach maturity value after 4 years. After the fourth year, interest is paid 3-monthly at a lower rate.

Non-income related benefits

Social Security benefits included in this category are:

Statutory Sick Pay

Statutory Maternity Pay

Disability Living Allowance

Child Benefit

Retirement Pension

Widowed Mother's Allowance

Widow's Payment

Widow's Pension

War Disablement Pension

War Widow's Pension

Severe Disablement Allowance

Attendance Allowance

Invalid Care Allowance

Jobseeker's Allowance (contribution based)

Industrial Injuries Disablement Benefit

Incapacity Benefit

Maternity Allowance

Guardian's Allowance

Occupational pension

Pensions received from schemes run by an employer. Employees may be a member of an employer's pension scheme on a voluntary basis. Occupational pension schemes can be contracted in to or out of *SERPS*. Most major employee schemes are contracted out.

Other bank/building society account

Accounts belonging to *adult*s recorded under categories "savings account, investment account/bond, any other account with bank building society, etc" plus *children*'s building society and bank accounts.

Pension mortgage

Similar to an *endowment* mortgage but is available only to the self employed and those who are not members of an *occupational pension* scheme.

Interest only is paid to the lender and monthly contributions are paid into a pension plan which is designed to repay the mortgage when the borrower retires.

In addition, it is necessary to arrange a separate term assurance policy designed to repay the mortgage if the borrower should die before the end of the mortgage term. The assurance policy serves the same purpose as a mortgage protection policy.

Payments to the pension plan and premiums on the assurance policy are not included as part of *Housing Costs*.

PEP

Personal Equity Plan. Managed investment of a lump sum or regular savings in the stock market. Any dividend earnings and growth in value is free of tax.

Pensioner benefit unit

Benefit units whose *Family status* is either *pensioner couple, single male or single female pensioner.*

Personal pension

Pensions received from schemes which a person has joined to save for an income in retirement and which is not run by either an employer or the State.

DSS, Family Resources Survey Great Britain 1999-2000, © Crown Copyright 2001

Post Office account

National Savings Bank/PO ordinary and investment accounts.

Premium Bonds

Investments which do not earn interest, but are entered in a monthly draw for tax-free money prizes.

Refundable Tax Credits

Disabled Person's Tax Credit

Working Families' Tax Credit

Rent free accommodation

Accommodation provided free by an employer, or by an organisation to a self employed respondent, provided that the normal activities of the informant are to further the cause of the organisation (eg Church of England clergy).

Accommodation is not rent free if anyone, apart from an employer or organisation, is paying a rent or mortgage on a property on behalf of the respondent.

Repayment mortgage

Money borrowed for the purchase of the house is repaid over a period of years; interest is also paid on the amount outstanding at the time. Usually the payments consist partly of repayments of the original loan and partly of interest.

Retirement Pension

Social Security benefit paid to women aged 60 or over and to men aged 65 or over. There are two categories of contributory Retirement Pension and two categories of non-contributory Retirement Pension. For more information see Social Security Statistics, (CDS, ISBN 1 84123 145 2).

Save As You Earn

A 5 or 7 year regular monthly savings scheme for employees. It can also be linked to a company share option scheme; at the end of the term the employee can either use the savings to buy the shares in their company, or take the accumulated investment.

The interest rate is fixed over the term, and interest is tax-free. SAYE ended in November 1994, but previous schemes remain valid.

Savings

Total value of all assets and investments. Figures are taken from responses to questions on the value of assets or estimated using information on interest. The introduction to Chapter 5 gives more information on the questions asked and data quality. Note banded savings do not include assets held by *children* in the *benefit unit/household*. The derivation of total savings used in the tables means that "no savings" specifically relates to cases where either respondents said they had no accounts/investments or that some accounts/investments were recorded but that none of them yielded any interest/dividends.

The full derivation of this variable is available on request from ASD3E, at the address listed in the Introduction.

SERPS

State Earnings Related Pension Scheme. Available to individuals who satisfy contributions conditions. It does not have to be claimed separately from the basic *Retirement Pension* and is not affected by the receipt of other income.

Calculation of benefit is by reference to earnings from 6 April 1978 or the start of working life, whichever is later.

Individuals can contract out of SERPS as part of an *occupational pension* scheme or *personal pension* scheme.

Severe Disablement Allowance

Social Security benefit provided for people who are incapable of work and do not satisfy the contributions conditions for *Incapacity Benefit*.

Claimants must be aged between 16 and 65 when they make their claim and must have been incapable of work for at least 28 weeks.

For more information see Social Security Statistics, (CDS, ISBN 1 84123 145 2).

Shared ownership schemes

Where the householder pays a mortgage and a rent on the same property. In these circumstances, both the rented and owner questions will be asked.

Sick or disabled adults

Adults below *state pension age* who have a long standing illness or are restricted in what they can do, or are registered disabled at a local authority.

Social class

Classification system which has grown out of the original Registrar General's social class classification based on responses to questions on occupation. FRS only collects this information for those currently in work or who have worked in the last 12 months.

Social Fund

Made up of regulated and discretionary payments. Maternity Funeral and Cold Weather Payments are governed by regulations. They are available to people who are on certain Social Security benefits and who meet various other conditions. The discretionary part of the Social Fund provides help in the form of non-repayable grants and interest-free loans. The discretionary payments are Community Care Grants, Budgeting Loans and Crisis Loans.

For more information see Social Security Statistics, (CDS, ISBN 1 84123 145 2).

Sources of income

Wages and salaries

For those currently working as an employee, income is equal to:

gross pay before any deductions,

less any refunds of income tax,

less any motoring and mileage expenses,

less any refunds for items of household expenditure,

plus bonuses received over the last 12 months (converted to a weekly amount),

less any SSP/SMP,

plus *children's* earnings from part time jobs.

Self employment income

This is the total amount of income received from self employment gross of tax and national insurance payments, based on profits where individual considers themselves as running a business, on estimated earnings/drawings otherwise.

Excludes any profit due to partners in the business.

Any losses are deducted.

Investments

Interest and dividends received on savings and investments:

Current accounts

DSS, Family Resources Survey Great Britain 1999-2000, © Crown Copyright 2001

Post Office accounts

Other bank/building society accounts

TESSAs

Gilts

PEPs

Unit trusts

Stocks and shares

ISAs

State Retirement Pension plus any Income Support

For *adults* over *state pension age,* any *Retirement Pension* and/or *Income Support* which is received.

These benefits are shown together because of known problems with reporting of amounts for pensioners.

Other pensions

Payments received from *occupational and personal pension* schemes; widow's employee pensions, trade union and friendly society pensions, annuity pensions, trusts and covenants.

Social Security disability benefits

Attendance Allowance

Disability Living Allowance

War Disablement Pension

Severe Disablement Allowance

Disability Working Allowance/Disabled Person's Tax Credit

Industrial Injuries Disablement Benefit

Incapacity Benefit

Other Social Security benefits

Extended Payment of *Council Tax Benefit*

Extended Payment of *Housing Benefit*

Back To Work Bonus

Housing Benefit

Income Support (for *Adults* under *state pension age*)

Family Credit/Working Families' Tax Credit

Council Tax Benefit

Child Benefit

Widowed Mother's Allowance

Widow's Payment

Widow's Pension

War Widow's Pension

Invalid Care Allowance

Jobseeker's Allowance

Statutory Sick Pay

Statutory Maternity Pay

Maternity Allowance

Guardian's Allowance

Social Fund Grant for Funeral Expenses

Social Fund Grant for Maternity Expenses

Community Care Grants

Any other State Benefits

Other sources

Income received as a baby-sitter

Income received as a mail order agent

Allowances from an absent spouse (including direct payments for household items)

Allowances from a spouse in the forces, friends, other relatives etc. outside the household

Allowances from an organisation

Allowances from a local authority for a foster child

Allowances from a local authority for an adopted child

Luncheon vouchers

Royalties

Income as a sleeping partner

Pension from an overseas Government (paid in foreign currency)

Maintenance

Income from odd jobs

Income from property

Income from sub-tenants

Income from those outside the household paying towards rents/mortgages

Educational grants

Student loans

Parental contributions to students

Free welfare milk, school meals and school milk (assigned to the head of the *benefit unit*)

Trade union sick or strike pay (other than that received in a lump sum)

Friendly society benefits (other than those received in a lump sum)

Benefits from unemployment/redundancy insurance (other than those received in a lump sum)

Benefits from private sickness schemes (other than those received in a lump sum)

Benefits from accident insurance (other than those received in a lump sum)

Benefits from hospital savings schemes (other than those received in a lump sum)

Benefits from permanent health insurance (other than those received in a lump sum)

Government training scheme allowances

plus *children's* income from Trusts

The full derivation of these variables are available on request from ASD3E, at the address listed in the Introduction.

State pension age

65 for men, 60 for women.

DSS, Family Resources Survey Great Britain 1999–2000, © Crown Copyright 2001

Stocks and shares

Includes bonds, debentures and other securities which are usually bought and sold on the financial markets. Bonds issued by foreign governments and local authorities are also recorded here.

A share is a single unit of ownership in a company. 'Stocks' is the general term for various types of security issued by companies to attract investment in the form of loans.

Tenure

Rented from Council

Includes all cases where the local authority is the landlord (except where accommodation is part of job), or where rented unfurnished property is owned by a New Town Development Corporation or the Scottish Special Housing Association.

Rented from Housing Association

Includes all housing associations except those under "rented from Council" and where accommodation is part of job.

Rented privately – furnished

Also includes *rent free* cases and those where information on whether property was furnished was missing.

Rented privately – unfurnished

Also includes cases where respondents were occupying their accommodation *rent free.*

Buying with a mortgage

Includes local authority and housing association part-own/part-rent and *co and shared ownership* arrangements.

Owned outright

Households who have paid off the mortgage or loan used to purchase the property. These *households* may have other loans secured on their property for which information is collected on the FRS. However, these payments are excluded from housing costs.

TESSA

Tax Exempt Special Savings Account. Usually arranged via a bank or building society. Lasts for 5 years and, provided the savings are left there for that time, interest earned will be tax free. Interest usually credited annually.

Unit trusts

A collective, managed investment in the financial markets. Investors buy 'units' of a fund that invests in *shares, stocks, Gilts*, etc. Interest (the 'dividend') is paid net of tax, usually half yearly.

War Disablement Pension

Social Security Benefit provided for people who were disabled in the Armed Forces between 1914 and 1921 or any time after 2 September 1939. Paid at a rate which varies according to the degree of disablement.

For more information see Social Security Statistics, (CDS, ISBN 1 84123 145 2).

War Widow's Pension

Social Security Benefit provided for widows of servicemen who died as a result of service in HM Forces. The standard rate of pension may be paid if the widow has a dependent child or is over 40 or is incapable of self support. The lower rate is paid to childless widows under the age of 40.

For more information see Social Security Statistics, (CDS, ISBN 1 84123 145 2).

Widow's Benefits

Widow's Benefits include the receipt of *Widow's Pension, Widowed Mother's Allowance* or *Widow's Payment.*

Widowed Mother's Allowance

Widows are eligible to NI Widow's benefits if her late husband met the contributions conditions. Widowed Mother's Allowance can be paid to a widow as long as she is entitled to *Child Benefit* for at least one qualifying child, or she is pregnant by her late husband, or in certain cases of artificial insemination. Child dependency increases are paid for each child. Note, Widow's Payment is not included with Widowed Mother's Allowance or Widow's Pension (figures are recorded under any other state benefit).

For more information see Social Security Statistics, (CDS, ISBN 1 84123 145 2).

Widow's Payment

Widows are eligible to widow's payments if her late husband satisfied the contributions conditions. Widows are also eligible if her late husband died as the result of an industrial injury or disease and she was under 60 when her late husband died, or if she was over 60 and he was not entitled to a Category A Retirement Pension when he died. The payment is a tax free lump sum of £1,000. This is converted into a weekly figure in sources of income tables.

For more information see Social Security Statistics, (CDS, ISBN 1 84123 145 2).

Widow's Pension

Widows are eligible to NI Widow's benefits if her late husband met the contributions conditions. A widow who is 45 or over when she stops being entitled to *Widowed Mother's Allowance,* or when she is widowed, can get Widow's Pension. If she is 55 or over at that time she will get the standard rate of benefit. Note, Widow's Payment is not included with Widowed Mother's Allowance or Widow's Pension (figures are recorded under any other state benefit).

For more information see Social Security Statistics, (CDS, ISBN 1 84123 145 2).

Working Families' Tax Credit

A tax credit payable to working families depending on their circumstances. It replaced family credit for awards starting the first week of October 1999. It is administered by the Inland Revenue. The claimant or partner must be working at least 16 hours per week.

For more information visit www.IR.Gov.UK

DSS, Family Resources Survey Great Britain 1999-2000, © Crown Copyright 2001

Family Resources Survey 1999-2000: Items covered

This list summarises the information that was collected on the 1999-2000 survey. Items are shown alphabetically within topics, largely in the order they appear on the questionnaire.

The second column indicates the level at which the question is asked. For example, household level questions will be asked once and refer to the whole household, whereas adult level questions will be asked of all, or a subset of, adult household members individually.

New items for 1999-2000 are shown in **bold**. For further information, please contact ASD3E at the address listed in the Introduction.

Topic	Level	Item
Household composition	Adult/Child	Age
Household composition	Adult/Child	Date of Birth (under 20s only)
Household composition	Adult	Ethnic group
Household composition	Adult	Full time education, age completed
Household composition	Adult/Child	Full time education, presently in
Household composition	Adult/Child	Full time education, school or college attended, type
Household composition	Adult	Legal marital status (whether cohabiting now part of household grid)
Household composition	Adult/Child	Relationship to other adults/children in household
Household composition	Adult/Child	Sex
Household composition	Adult	Widowed, age when
Household composition	Adult	Widowed, number of children under 16 when
Tenure	Household	Accommodation, type (detached, semi-detached, terraced, purpose-built flat etc)
Tenure	Household	Floor, level of accommodation
Tenure	Household	Household, status (conventional, shared)
Tenure	Head of Household	Lived at address, months (if less than one year)
Tenure	Head of Household	Lived at address, years
Tenure	Adult	Property owned or rented, in whose name
Tenure	Household	Rooms
Tenure	Household	Rooms, bedrooms
Tenure	Household	Rooms, for business
Tenure	Household	Rooms, only for business
Tenure	Household	Rooms, partly for business
Tenure	Household	Rooms, shared with non-household members
Tenure	Household	Sublet, formal arrangements to
Tenure	Household	Sublet, who to (close relative, other relative, non-relative)
Tenure	Household	Tenure
Tenure	Household	Tenure, shared ownership, whether paid off mortgage element
Tenure/rented accommodation	Household	Furnished or unfurnished accommodation
Tenure/rented accommodation	Household	Landlord
Tenure/rented accommodation	Household	Landlord, lives in building
Tenure/rented accommodation	Household	Landlord, same flat
Tenure/rented accommodation	Household	Tenancy, agreement (written, unwritten)
Tenure/rented accommodation	Household	Tenancy, agreement type (assured shorthold, shorthold)
Tenure/rented accommodation	Household	Tenancy, date first became tenants (1988 or earlier/1989 onwards)
Tenure/rented accommodation	Household	Tenancy, other ways of letting accommodation (company licence, college licence, non-exclusive occupancy agreement, holiday let, low season let)
Tenure/rented accommodation	Household	Tenancy, registered as a fair rent
Tenure/rented accommodation	Household	Tied accommodation, with present job of anyone in household
Tenure/rented accommodation	Adult	Tied accommodation, with present job of anyone in household; which member
Rent/rented accommodation	Benefit unit	Amount paid
Rent/rented accommodation	Up to 5 payments per household	Amount paid by someone outside household (DSS, Employer, other organisation, friend or relative, other)
Rent/rented accommodation	Up to 5 payments per household	Amount paid by someone outside household, period covered
Rent/rented accommodation	Benefit unit	Amount paid, period covered
Rent/rented accommodation	Benefit unit	Full rent, before Housing Benefit
Rent/rented accommodation	Household	Rent free weeks
Rent/rented accommodation	Household	Services (lighting, heating, hot water, fuel), amount included in rent
Rent/rented accommodation	Household	Water/sewerage charges, amount included in rent
Rent/rented accommodation	Household	Whether have documentation to consult
Housing Benefit	Benefit unit	Amount received
Housing Benefit	Benefit unit	Amount received, period covered
Housing Benefit	Household	Amount received, includes extra allowance for child care expenses
Housing Benefit	Household	In receipt, 100% rebate
Housing Benefit	Household	In receipt, directly or paid to landlord

Housing Benefit	Benefit unit	Number of weeks in receipt this time
Housing Benefit	Benefit unit	Rent rebate or rent allowance, awaiting outcome of a claim
Housing Benefit	Household	Statement from council, amount of eligible rent
Housing Benefit	Household	Statement from council, amount of eligible rent, period covered
Mortgages/owner occupied accommodation	Household	Number of loans taken out to purchase accommodation
Mortgages/owner occupied accommodation	Up to 3 mortgages per household	Amount outstanding on current mortgage/loan
Mortgages/owner occupied accommodation	Up to 4 per mortgage	Endowment/pension plan/PEP/unit trust, amount of last premium
Mortgages/owner occupied accommodation	Up to 4 per mortgage	Endowment/pension plan/PEP/unit trust, amount of last premium, period covered
Mortgages/owner occupied accommodation	Up to 4 per mortgage	Endowment, year taken out
Mortgages/owner occupied accommodation	Up to 3 mortgages per household	Flexible mortgage, whether mortgage of this type
Mortgages/owner occupied accommodation	Up to 3 mortgages per household	Interest paid on mortgage/loan
Mortgages/owner occupied accommodation	Up to 3 mortgages per household	Interest paid on mortgage/loan, period covered
Mortgages/owner occupied accommodation	Up to 3 mortgages per household	Lender (building society, bank, other)
Mortgages/owner occupied accommodation	Up to 3 mortgages per household	MIRAS tax relief deducted
Mortgages/owner occupied accommodation	Up to 3 per mortgage	Mortgage protection policy, amount of last payment
Mortgages/owner occupied accommodation	Up to 3 per mortgage	Mortgage protection policy, amount of last payment, period covered
Mortgages/owner occupied accommodation	Up to 3 per mortgage	Mortgage protection policy, year taken out
Mortgages/owner occupied accommodation	Up to 3 per mortgage	Mortgage protection policy, what covered
Mortgages/owner occupied accommodation	Up to 3 mortgages per household	Original loan, amount
Mortgages/owner occupied accommodation	Up to 6 per mortgage	Payments made by someone outside household, amount paid
Mortgages/owner occupied accommodation	Up to 6 per mortgage	Payments made by someone outside household, payee (DSS, Employer, other organisation, friend/relative, mortgage protection/insurance policy, other)
Mortgages/owner occupied accommodation	Up to 6 per mortgage	Payments made by someone outside household, period covered
Mortgages/owner occupied accommodation	Up to 3 mortgages per household	Purchase price
Mortgages/owner occupied accommodation	Up to 3 mortgages per household	Remortgage, amount
Mortgages/owner occupied accommodation	Up to 3 mortgages per household	Remortgage, reasons for
Mortgages/owner occupied accommodation	Up to 3 mortgages per household	Remortgage, year taken out
Mortgages/owner occupied accommodation	Up to 3 mortgages per household	Repayment mortgage, amount of interest charged in last 12 months
Mortgages/owner occupied accommodation	Up to 3 mortgages per household	Repayment mortgage, last instalment
Mortgages/owner occupied accommodation	Up to 3 mortgages per household	Repayment mortgage, last instalment, period covered
Mortgages/owner occupied accommodation	Household	Right to buy, where house bought after 1980, whether been renting the property before decided to buy it
Mortgages/owner occupied accommodation	Household	Right to buy, where house bought after 1980, whether been renting the property before decided to buy it, who rented from
Mortgages/owner occupied accommodation	Up to 3 mortgages per household	Second mortgage, reasons for
Mortgages/owner occupied accommodation	Up to 3 mortgages per household	Type (endowment, repayment, pension, PEP, unit trust, both an endowment or any other interest only mortgage and a repayment mortgage)
Mortgages/owner occupied accommodation	Up to 3 mortgages per household	Year in which mortgage/loan is taken out
Mortgages/owner occupied accommodation	Up to 3 mortgages per household	Year mortgage due to be paid off
Charges/owner occupied accommodation	Household	Type (ground rent, feu duties, chief rent, service charges, maintenance charges, site rent, factoring (payments to a land steward), other regular payments)
Charges/owner occupier accommodation	Household	Amount paid
Charges/owner occupier accommodation	Household	Amount paid, period covered
Structure and contents insurance	Household	Amount of premium (complete information for structural insurance only)
Structure and contents insurance	Household	Amount of premium, period covered
Structure and contents insurance	Household	Categories covered (structure only, furniture and contents only, both)
Council Tax	Household	Amount of last payment
Council Tax	Household	Amount of last payment, instalment or full year
Council Tax	Household	Amount of last payment equal to zero, why no Council Tax paid
Council Tax	Household	Annual amount on statement
Council Tax	Household	Annual amount on statement, amount included for Council Tax Water Charge (Scotland)
Council Tax	Household	Band
Council Tax	Household	Discount allowed (25 or 50%)
Council Tax	Household	Document/payment book consulted
Council Tax	Household	Lower valuation band because of disabled person in household
Council Tax	Household	Type of rebate/benefit, amount allowed
Council Tax	Household	Type of rebate/benefit, amount allowed, period covered
Council Tax	Household	Type of rebate/benefit, amount allowed, includes extra allowance for child care expenses
Council Tax	Household	Type of rebate/benefit, awaiting outcome of claim
Council Tax	Adult	Who rebate/benefit is for (according to statement)
Sewerage and mains water supply	Household	Sewerage rates, amount paid last time (where not included in rent or HB)
Sewerage and mains water supply	Household	Sewerage rates, number of times paid a year
Sewerage and mains water supply	Household	Water rates, amount paid last time (where not included in rent or HB)
Sewerage and mains water supply	Household	Water rates, number of times paid a year
Sewerage and mains water supply	Household	Whether pay separate or combined water and sewerage rates
Intra-household contributions	Adult	Amount of regular contribution, period covered
Intra-household contributions	Adult	Amount of rent paid

Intra-household contributions	Adult	Amount of rent paid, heating included or paid separately
Intra-household contributions	Adult	Amount of rent paid, period covered
Intra-household contributions	Adult	Housing Benefit, amount received by second and subsequent benefit units (now asked on the individual schedule)
Intra-household contributions	Adult	Housing Benefit, amount received by second and subsequent benefit units, period covered (now asked on the individual schedule)
Intra-household contributions	Adult	Housing Benefit, amount received by second and subsequent benefit units, number of weeks in receipt this time
Intra-household contributions	Adult	Housing Benefit, amount received by second and subsequent benefit units, whether awaiting the outcome of a claim
Intra-household contributions	Adult	Status of adult (boarder, lodger, other)
Income from property	Adult	Sub-letting, income received in last 12 months before deduction of income tax
Income from property	Adult	Rent received from other property in the last 12 months, after paying for repairs, loan interest, rent, rates, property insurance, legal costs and maintenance costs
Insurance policies	Up to 6 policies per household	Any members of household have insurance policies
Insurance policies	Up to 6 policies per household	Person insured
Insurance policies	Up to 6 policies per household	Person who pays premiums (person insured or someone else)
Insurance policies	Up to 6 policies per household	Type of cover (personal accident, private medical treatment, redundancy, loss salary or earnings due to ill health)
Insurance policies	Up to 6 policies per household	Value of the last premium
Consumer durables	Household	Access to durable items (washing machine, tumble drier, fridge/freezer, refrigerator, deep freeze, microwave, cooker, dishwasher, TV, video, telephone, home computer, compact disc player, satellite dish/cable receiver)
Consumer durables	Household	Access to TV, whether there is one or more
Consumer durables	Household	Central heating in accommodation, including storage heaters
Consumer durables	Household	Central heating, fuel used (electricity, mains gas, solid fuel, oil etc)
Vehicles	Up to 8 vehicles per Benefit Unit	Arrangement of use (owned or continuous use)
Vehicles	Household	Number in household
Vehicles	Up to 8 vehicles per Benefit Unit	Type (car, light van, motorcycle, other)
Welfare/school milk/meals	Child	School meals, number received in last 7 days
Welfare/school milk/meals	Child	School milk, cartons received in last 7 days
Welfare/school milk/meals	Adult/Child	Welfare milk, pints received in last 7 days
Children aged 16-24 outside household	Household	Children outside household who receive full or part time education
Children aged 16-24 outside household	Up to 4 per household	Children outside household who receive full or part time education, amount paid in fees or maintenance for educational courses in last 12 months
Children aged 16-24 outside household	Up to 4 per household	Children outside household who receive full or part time education, amount paid in fees or maintenance for educational courses in last 12 months, period covered
Children aged 16-24 outside household	Up to 4 per household	Children outside household who receive full or part time education, parents
Childcare	Child	Childminder/nursery registered
Childcare	Child	Cost per week for child, holidays
Childcare	Child	Cost per week for child, term time
Childcare	Child	Does anyone care for child whilst parent is working
Childcare	Child	Hours a week, holidays
Childcare	Child	Hours a week, term time
Childcare	Child	Other arrangement (payment in kind, exchange basis, vouchers under the Nursery Education Vouchers Scheme, other, no cost/payment)
Childcare	Child	Who looks after child(close/other relative, friend/neighbour, childminder, Nursery/ playgroup, crèche, other)
Informal care	**Adult/Children**	Person giving help, average hours a week **(banded)** spent giving care to person needing it
Informal care	Adult/Children	Person giving help (children in household taken as one group; also includes categories for relatives, friends/neighbours, other outside helpers)
Informal care	Adult/Child	Person needing help (also includes categories for non-household members)
Informal care	Adult/Children	Person needing help, frequency of help given (continuously, several times a day etc)
Health restrictions on work	Adult	Restriction in amount and type of work due to injury, illness or disability
Health restrictions on work	Adult	Period unable to work due to injury, illness or disability (28 weeks or less, 28 weeks up to 1 year, more than 1 year)
Health restrictions on work	Adult	Period unable to work due to injury, illness or disability, more than 1 year, which year
Health restrictions on work	Adult	Hours able to work a week (whether currently employed or not)
Health restrictions on work	Adult	Long-standing illness, disability or infirmity (harmonised)
Health restrictions on work	Adult	Long-standing illness, disability or infirmity, whether limits activities
Health restrictions on work	Adult	Prevented from seeking work due to disability or illness, caring for disabled/elderly person, looking after child(ren)
Health restrictions on work	Adult	Prevented from seeking work due to disability or illness, caring for disabled/elderly person, looking after child(ren), person being cared for (including non-household members)
Health restrictions on work	Adult	Registered disabled with local authority
Health restrictions on work	Adult	Registered disabled with local authority, categories (blind, partially sighted, deaf)
Children's health	Child	Long-standing illness (period of at least 6 months)

Children's health	Child	Long-standing illness, whether limits activities
Educational and work related qualifications	Adult	Any educational qualifications for which certificate received
Educational and work related qualifications	Adult	Any educational qualifications for which certificate received, highest qualification
Educational and work related qualifications	Adult	Any professional, vocational or other work related qualifications for which certificate received
Educational and work related qualifications	Adult	Any professional, vocational or other work related qualifications for which certificate received, highest qualification
Educational grants/loans	Adult	Access funds, whether receiving any regular payment
Educational grants/loans	Adult	Access funds, whether receiving any regular payment, amount received
Educational grants/loans	Adult	Access funds, whether receiving any regular payment, amount received, period covered
Educational grants/loans	Household	Anyone in household attending course for which receive educational grant or scholarship
Educational grants/loans	Up to 2 grants per adult/child	Grant, amount paid directly to student
Educational grants/loans	Up to 2 grants per adult/child	Grant, current annual value, excluding fees
Educational grants/loans	Up to 2 grants per adult/child	Grant, current annual value, including fees
Educational grants/loans	Adult/Child	Grant, number received
Educational grants/loans	Adult/Child	Grant, person receiving, grant or scholarship
Educational grants/loans	Up to 2 grants per adult/child	Grant, source (state, private or overseas)
Educational grants/loans	Up to 2 loans per adult/child	Loan, amount entitled to borrow under top up loan scheme
Educational grants/loans	Up to 2 loans per adult	Loan, amount of last repayment
Educational grants/loans	Up to 2 loans per adult	Loan, amount of last repayment, period covered
Educational grants/loans	Up to 2 loans per adult	Loan, amount originally borrowed
Educational grants/loans	Up to 2 loans per adult	Loan, inclusion of last payment (just capital or some repayment of capital)
Educational grants/loans	Up to 2 loans per adult	Loan, interest (carry interest or interest free)
Educational grants/loans	Up to 2 loans per adult	Loan, lender (organisation or individual person)
Educational grants/loans	Up to 2 loans per adult	Loan, number (one, two, three or more)
Educational grants/loans	Adult	Loan, person eligible for loan
Educational grants/loans	Up to 2 loans per adult	Loan, total amount borrowed during academic year
Educational grants/loans	Up to 2 loans per adult	Loan, year taken out
Educational grants/loans	Adult	Presently receiving full/part time education (other than leisure classes), amount of any parental contribution in last 12 months
Educational grants/loans	Adult	Presently receiving full/part time education (other than leisure classes), amount of any parental contribution in last 12 months, period covered
Educational grants/loans	Adult/child	Students receiving grants, year in which course started
Educational grants/loans	Adult/child	Students receiving grants, year in which course will end
Educational grants/loans	Adult	Top up loan from Student Loan Company, amount borrowed during academic year
Educational grants/loans	Adult	Whether have been a student at any time since 1990
Educational grants/loans	Adult	Whether have made repayments to Student loan from Student Loan Company in last 12 months
Employment status	Adult	Absent from work for more than the last 3 working days
Employment status	Adult	Absent from work for more than the last 3 working days, days absent (if less than 1 week)
Employment status	Adult	Absent from work for more than the last 3 working days, on full, part or no pay
Employment status	Adult	Absent from work for more than the last 3 working days, reason for absence
Employment status	Adult	Absent from work for more than the last 3 working days, weeks absent
Employment status	Adult	Any paid work in the last 7 days
Employment status	Adult	Away from job/business in last 7 days
Employment status	Adult	Employment status (employee or self employed)
Employment status	Adult	Full/part time: respondent's assessment
Employment status	Adult	Government training scheme, able to start within 2 weeks had one been available
Employment status	Adult	Government training scheme, type attended (Youth Training, Training for Work, Work Trial, Project Work, Career Development Loans, New Deal for 18-24 year olds, any other training scheme, none of these)
Employment status	Adult	Government training scheme, type attended, New Deal for 18-24 year olds, New Deal option (The Gateway, employment option, full time education or training, voluntary sector, environmental task force)
Employment status	Adult	Length of time in present job (employee/self employed)
Employment status	Adult	Looking for paid work or government training scheme in last 4 weeks
Employment status	Adult	Main reason did not want work in last 4 weeks
Employment status	Adult	Main reason for not looking for work in last 4 weeks
Employment status	Adult	Month last did any paid work
Employment status	Adult	Number of jobs held
Employment status	Adult	Presently receiving full/part time education (other than leisure classes)
Employment status	Adult	Presently receiving full/part time education (other than leisure classes), hours per week receiving tuition (lectures, practicals, seminars)
Employment status	Adult	Presently receiving full/part time education (other than leisure classes), hours spent studying: daytime, evenings or both
Employment status	Adult	Retired within last 12 months
Employment status	Adult	Retired within last 12 months, amount earned in last 12 months before retirement
Employment status	**Adult**	**Retired within last 12 months, month retired**
Employment status	**Adult**	**Retired within last 12 months, reason for retiring below state pension age (ill-health, compulsory, time with family etc)**
Employment status	Adult	Seeking work, full time or part time or no preference

DSS, Family Resources Survey Great Britain 1999-2000, © Crown Copyright 2001

Employment status	Adult	Seeking work, full time or part time or no preference, hours meant by full time
Employment status	Adult	Signed on at Unemployment Benefit office or Jobcentre in last week
Employment status	Adult	Unpaid work, whether did any in last 7 days in business you or a relative owns
Employment status	Adult	Weeks regular paid work in last 12 months
Employment status	Adult	Would like a regular paid job
Employment status	Adult	Worked, or going to work, today
Employment status	Adult	Ever had paid work
Employment status	Adult	When last paid work was done
Employment status	Adult	Year last did any paid work
Employment status	Adult	Years spent in full time work since finishing continuous education
Employment status	Adult	Years spent in part time work since finishing continuous education
Job description	Subset of Adults	Occupational coding (SOC)
Job description	Subset of Adults	Social Class
Employee pay details	Up to 3 jobs per adult	Able to work more hours if suitable childcare were available
Employee pay details	Up to 3 jobs per adult	AVCs, amount deducted from last pay
Employee pay details	Up to 3 jobs per adult	Amount of pay received last time, whether usual
Employee pay details	Up to 3 jobs per adult	Amount received last time (including bonus, overtime or tips)
Employee pay details	Up to 3 jobs per adult	Amount received last time, period covered
Employee pay details	Up to 3 jobs per adult	Amount usually received after all deductions (where last pay not usual)
Employee pay details	Up to 3 jobs per adult	Amount usually received before all deductions (where last pay not usual)
Employee pay details	Up to 3 jobs per adult	Amount usually received before all deductions (where last pay not usual), period covered
Employee pay details	Up to 3 jobs per adult	Amount usually received, amount included for motoring
Employee pay details	Up to 3 jobs per adult	Benefits received from present employer (free or subsidised canteen, goods, medical insurance, share options, payment of school fees, childcare provision and/or vouchers, provision of a phone, luncheon vouchers)
Employee pay details	Up to 6 bonuses per job	Bonus, amount (before tax, after tax)
Employee pay details	Up to 6 bonuses per job	Bonus, amount included in usual pay
Employee pay details	Up to 3 jobs per adult	Bonus, number received in last 12 months
Employee pay details	Up to 6 bonuses per job	Bonus, whether included in usual pay (where last pay not usual)
Employee pay details	Up to 3 jobs per adult	Charity, amount deducted from last pay
Employee pay details	Up to 3 jobs per adult	Contracted hours, happy with hours (or more or less)
Employee pay details	Up to 3 jobs per adult	Contracted hours, weekly
Employee pay details	Up to 3 jobs per adult	Date last paid
Employee pay details	Up to 3 jobs per adult	Friendly societies, amount deducted from last pay
Employee pay details	Up to 3 jobs per adult	Gross earnings this year (where payslip consulted)
Employee pay details	Up to 3 jobs per adult	Gross wage (where payslip consulted)
Employee pay details	Main job	Mileage allowance, amount included in last pay
Employee pay details	Up to 3 jobs per adult	National Insurance normally paid (where deduction is zero)
Employee pay details	Up to 3 jobs per adult	National Insurance, amount deducted from last pay
Employee pay details	Up to 3 jobs per adult	Other deductions, amount deducted from last pay
Employee pay details	Up to 3 jobs per adult	Overtime, average hours, weekly
Employee pay details	Up to 3 jobs per adult	PAYE, amount deducted from last pay
Employee pay details	Up to 3 jobs per adult	Payslip consulted
Employee pay details	Up to 3 jobs per adult	Pension or superannuation, amount deducted from last pay
Employee pay details	Up to 3 jobs per adult	Prevented working more hours, person being cared for
Employee pay details	Up to 3 jobs per adult	Prevented working more hours, reasons
Employee pay details	Main job	Refund of income tax, amount included in last pay
Employee pay details	Main job	Refund of motoring expenses, amount included in last pay
Employee pay details	Main job	Refunds of household expenditure, amount included in last pay
Employee pay details	Up to 3 jobs per adult	Repayment of loan, amount deducted from last salary
Employee pay details	Up to 3 jobs per adult	SMP, made up pay
Employee pay details	Up to 3 jobs per adult	SMP, weeks stopped work before baby was born
Employee pay details	Up to 3 jobs per adult	Sports clubs, specialist past times, amount deducted from last pay
Employee pay details	Up to 3 jobs per adult	SSP, made up pay
Employee pay details	Main job	SSP/SMP, amount included in last pay
Employee pay details	Up to 3 jobs per adult	Union fees, amount deducted from last pay
Self employed earnings	Up to 3 jobs per adult	Able to work more hours if suitable childcare were available
Self employed earnings	Up to 3 jobs per adult	Any other income from job/business for personal use, apart from any drawings from the bank/building society, average amount taken out each month
Self employed earnings	Up to 3 jobs per adult	Business accounts, whether prepared for the Inland Revenue for tax purposes
Self employed earnings	Up to 3 jobs per adult	Business status (sole or partnership)
Self employed earnings	Up to 3 jobs per adult	Business status, whether think of self more as having a job or a business (used for subsequent questions, description most applicable to the respondent)
Self employed earnings	Up to 3 jobs per adult	Date ceased being self employed
Self employed earnings	Up to 3 jobs per adult	Drawings from work account, average amount taken out each month for non-business purposes
Self employed earnings	Up to 3 jobs per adult	Happy with hours (or more or less)
Self employed earnings	Up to 3 jobs per adult	Hours worked a week (self employed)
Self employed earnings	Up to 3 jobs per adult	Income from job/business, average weekly/monthly amount over the last 12 months
Self employed earnings	Up to 3 jobs per adult	Income from job/business, average weekly/monthly amount over the last 12 months, amount of income tax deducted last time
Self employed earnings	Up to 3 jobs per adult	Income from job/business, average weekly/monthly amount over the last 12 months,

		amount of income tax deducted last time, period covered
Self employed earnings	Up to 3 jobs per adult	Income from job/business, average weekly/monthly amount over the last 12 months, amount of National Insurance deducted last time
Self employed earnings	Up to 3 jobs per adult	Income from job/business, average weekly/monthly amount over the last 12 months, amount of National Insurance deducted last time, period covered
Self employed earnings	Up to 3 jobs per adult	Income from job/business, average weekly/monthly amount over the last 12 months, whether income tax or regular National Insurance contributions are deducted at source
Self employed earnings	Up to 3 jobs per adult	Income tax payment in connection with self employment, amount paid in last 12 months
Self employed earnings	Up to 3 jobs per adult	Income tax payment in connection with self employment, amount paid in last 12 months, whether includes lump sum NI
Self employed earnings	Up to 3 jobs per adult	Lump sum NI in connection with self employment, amount paid in last 12 months
Self employed earnings	Up to 3 jobs per adult	Number of weeks self employed in last 12 months
Self employed earnings	Up to 3 jobs per adult	Prevented working more hours, person being cared for
Self employed earnings	Up to 3 jobs per adult	Prevented working more hours, reasons
Self employed earnings	Up to 3 jobs per adult	Profit/loss, amount before tax and lump sum National Insurance deductions
Self employed earnings	Up to 3 jobs per adult	Profit/loss shown on business accounts, amount
Self employed earnings	Up to 3 jobs per adult	Profit/loss shown on business accounts, amount not given, reasons (documents with accountant/Inland Revenue, other)
Self employed earnings	Up to 3 jobs per adult	Profit/loss shown on business accounts, document consulted
Self employed earnings	Up to 3 jobs per adult	Profit/loss shown on business accounts, end date of period
Self employed earnings	Up to 3 jobs per adult	Profit/loss shown on business accounts, start date of period
Self employed earnings	Up to 3 jobs per adult	Profit/loss shown on business accounts, whether before or after deduction of income tax
Self employed earnings	Up to 3 jobs per adult	Profit/loss shown on business accounts, whether before or after payment of any lump sum (Class 4) National Insurance payments based on taxable profits
Self employed earnings	Up to 3 jobs per adult	Regular National Insurance in connection with self employment, amount paid
Self employed earnings	Up to 3 jobs per adult	Regular National Insurance in connection with self employment, amount paid, period covered
Self employed earnings	Up to 3 jobs per adult	Separate bank or building society accounts for work and private finances
Pension schemes	Adult	Employer's pension scheme, whether make any AVCs
Pension schemes	Adult	Employer's pension scheme, whether make any AVCs, through employer or free standing
Pension schemes	Adult	Employer's pension scheme, current membership
Pension schemes	Adult	Employer's pension scheme, how long belonged
Pension schemes	Adult	Employer's pension scheme, if to leave job, whether still possible to make contributions
Pension schemes	Adult	Employer's pension scheme, type of pension (contributory, non-contributory)
Pension schemes	**Up to 3 personal pensions per adult**	Personal pension, age at which expect to start drawing pension
Pension schemes	**Up to 3 personal pensions per adult**	Personal pension, any contributions made in last 12 months by respondent, DSS, employer (or no contributions made)
Pension schemes	**Up to 3 personal pensions per adult**	Personal pension, contributions made in last 12 months by respondent, amount contributed last time
Pension schemes	**Up to 3 personal pensions per adult**	Personal pension, contributions made in last 12 months by respondent, amount contributed last time, period covered
Pension schemes	**Up to 3 personal pensions per adult**	Personal pension, currently have/making contributions
Pension schemes	**Up to 3 personal pensions per adult**	Personal pension, date started
Pension schemes	Adult	Personal pension, number currently have
Pension schemes	**Up to 3 personal pensions per adult**	**Personal pension, contracted out of SERPS**
Benefits	Adult	Any NI or State Benefit not specifically mentioned, received in the last 6 months
Benefits	Adult	Any NI or State Benefit not specifically mentioned, received in the last 6 months, currently receiving
Benefits	Adult	Any NI or State Benefit not specifically mentioned, received in the last 6 months, currently receiving, number of weeks received in last 6 months
Benefits	Adult	Attendance Allowance, amount received
Benefits	Adult	Attendance Allowance, amount received, period covered
Benefits	Adult	Attendance Allowance, anyone receiving Invalid Care Allowance
Benefits	Adult	Attendance Allowance, awarded to start at future date
Benefits	Adult	Attendance Allowance, how benefit paid (order book, giro cheque etc)
Benefits	Adult	Attendance Allowance, how benefit paid, paid as part of Retirement Pension
Benefits	Adult	Attendance Allowance, person(s) being cared for
Benefits	Adult	Back To Work Bonus (from October 1996), amount received in last 6 months
Benefits	Adult	Back To Work Bonus (from October 1996), whether building up a Bonus
Benefits	Adult	Back to Work Bonus (from October 1996), whether building up a Bonus, amount shown on statement for total accrued
Benefits	Adult	Benefits under accident insurance received in the last 12 months
Benefits	Adult	Benefits under accident insurance received in the last 12 months, presently receiving
Benefits	Adult	Benefits under accident insurance received in the last 12 months, presently receiving, amount received
Benefits	Adult	Benefits under accident insurance received in the last 12 months, presently receiving, amount received, period covered
Benefits	Adult	Benefits under accident insurance received in the last 12 months, presently receiving, number of weeks in last 12 months received
Benefits	Adult	Benefits under hospital savings scheme received in the last 12 months
Benefits	Adult	Benefits under hospital savings scheme received in the last 12 months, presently receiving
Benefits	Adult	Benefits under hospital savings scheme received in the last 12 months, presently receiving, amount received
Benefits	Adult	Benefits under hospital savings scheme received in the last 12 months, presently

DSS, Family Resources Survey Great Britain 1999-2000, © Crown Copyright 2001

		receiving, amount received, period covered
Benefits	Adult	Benefits under hospital savings scheme received in the last 12 months, presently receiving, number of weeks in last 12 months received
Benefits	Adult	Benefits under private sickness scheme received in the last 12 months
Benefits	Adult	Benefits under private sickness scheme received in the last 12 months, presently receiving
Benefits	Adult	Benefits under private sickness scheme received in the last 12 months, presently receiving, amount received
Benefits	Adult	Benefits under private sickness scheme received in the last 12 months, presently receiving, amount received, period covered
Benefits	Adult	Benefits under private sickness scheme received in the last 12 months, presently receiving, number of weeks in last 12 months received
Benefits	Adult	Benefits under redundancy/unemployment insurance scheme received in the last 12 months
Benefits	Adult	Benefits under redundancy/unemployment insurance scheme received in the last 12 months, presently receiving
Benefits	Adult	Benefits under redundancy/unemployment insurance scheme received in the last 12 months, presently receiving, amount received
Benefits	Adult	Benefits under redundancy/unemployment insurance received in the last 12 months, presently receiving, amount received, period covered
Benefits	Adult	Benefits under redundancy/unemployment insurance received in the last 12 months, presently receiving, number of weeks in last 12 months received
Benefits	Adult	Child Benefit, amount received
Benefits	Adult	Child Benefit, amount received, period covered
Benefits	Adult	Child Benefit, how benefit paid (order book, giro etc)
Benefits	Adult	Disability Living Allowance, care component, amount received
Benefits	Adult	Disability Living Allowance, care component, amount received, period covered
Benefits	Adult	Disability Living Allowance, care component, anyone receiving Invalid Care Allowance
Benefits	Adult	Disability Living Allowance, care component, awarded to start at future date
Benefits	Adult	Disability Living Allowance, care component, how benefit paid (order book, giro etc)
Benefits	Adult	Disability Living Allowance, care component, how benefit paid, paid as part of Retirement Pension
Benefits	Adult	Disability Living Allowance, care component, person(s) being received for
Benefits	Adult	Disability Living Allowance, mobility component, amount received
Benefits	Adult	Disability Living Allowance, mobility component, amount received, period covered
Benefits	Adult	Disability Living Allowance, mobility component, awarded to start at future date
Benefits	Adult	Disability Living Allowance, mobility component, how benefit paid (order book, giro etc)
Benefits	Adult	Disability Living Allowance, mobility component, how benefit paid, paid as part of Retirement Pension
Benefits	Adult	Disability Living Allowance, mobility component, person(s) being received for
Benefits	**Adult**	Disability Working Allowance/**Disabled Person's Tax Credit**, amount received
Benefits	**Adult**	Disability Working Allowance/**Disabled Person's Tax Credit**, amount received, includes extra allowance for child care expenses
Benefits	**Adult**	Disability Working Allowance/**Disabled Person's Tax Credit**, amount received, period covered
Benefits	**Adult**	Disability Working Allowance/**Disabled Person's Tax Credit**, how benefit paid (order book, giro etc)
Benefits	Adult	DSS direct payments (for mortgage interest, rent arrears, water charges, gas and electricity) total amount paid
Benefits	Adult	DSS direct payments (for mortgage interest, rent arrears, water charges, gas and electricity) total amount paid, period covered
Benefits	Adult	Extended Payment for Council Tax Benefit, whether received in last 6 months
Benefits	Adult	Extended Payment for Council Tax Benefit, whether received in last 6 months, amount received
Benefits	Adult	Extended Payment for Housing Benefit, whether received in last 6 months
Benefits	Adult	Extended Payment for Housing Benefit, whether received in last 6 months, amount received
Benefits	**Adult**	Family Credit/**Working Families' Tax Credit** lump sum paid in the last 6 months
Benefits	**Adult**	Family Credit/**Working Families' Tax Credit**, amount received
Benefits	**Adult**	Family Credit/**Working Families' Tax Credit**, how benefit paid (order book, giro etc)
Benefits	**Adult**	Family Credit/**Working Families' Tax Credit**, amount received, includes extra allowance for child care expenses
Benefits	**Adult**	Family Credit/**Working Families' Tax Credit**, amount received, period covered
Benefits	**Adult**	Family Credit/**Working Families' Tax Credit**, awaiting outcome of a claim
Benefits	**Adult**	Family Credit/**Working Families' Tax Credit**, lump sum paid in the last 6 months, amount received
Benefits	**Adult**	Family Credit/**Working Families' Tax Credit**, lump sum paid in the last 6 months, amount received, includes extra allowance for child care expenses
Benefits	**Adult**	Family Credit/**Working Families' Tax Credit**, number of weeks in continuous receipt
Benefits	Adult	Friendly Society Benefits received in the last 12 months
Benefits	Adult	Friendly Society Benefits received in the last 12 months, presently receiving
Benefits	Adult	Friendly Society Benefits received in the last 12 months, presently receiving, amount received
Benefits	Adult	Friendly Society Benefits received in the last 12 months, presently receiving, amount received, period covered
Benefits	Adult	Friendly Society Benefits received in the last 12 months, presently receiving, number of weeks in last 12 months received
Benefits	Adult	Government training scheme, allowance received
Benefits	Adult	Government training scheme, allowance received, period covered
Benefits	Adult	Guardian's Allowance, amount received
Benefits	Adult	Guardian's Allowance, amount received, period covered

Benefits	Adult	Guardian's Allowance, how benefit paid (order book, giro etc)
Benefits	Adult	Income Support, amount received
Benefits	Adult	Income Support, amount received, period covered
Benefits	Adult	Income Support, awaiting outcome of a claim
Benefits	Adult	Income Support, how benefit paid (order book, giro etc)
Benefits	Adult	Income Support, usual amount
Benefits	Adult	Income Support, weeks in receipt
Benefits	Adult	Income Support, whether includes any payment from CSA
Benefits	Adult	Industrial Injury Disablement Benefit, amount received
Benefits	Adult	Industrial Injury Disablement Benefit, amount received, period covered
Benefits	Adult	Industrial Injury Disablement Benefit, awaiting outcome of a claim
Benefits	Adult	Industrial Injury Disablement Benefit, how benefit paid (order book, giro etc)
Benefits	Adult	Invalid Care Allowance, amount received
Benefits	Adult	Invalid Care Allowance, amount received, period covered
Benefits	Adult	Invalid Care Allowance, how benefit paid (order book, giro etc)
Benefits	Adult	Invalid Care Allowance, person being cared for
Benefits	Adult	Incapacity Benefit, amount received
Benefits	Adult	Incapacity Benefit, amount received, period covered
Benefits	Adult	Incapacity Benefit, awaiting outcome of a claim
Benefits	Adult	Incapacity Benefit, how benefit paid (order book, giro etc)
Benefits	Adult	Incapacity Benefit, receiving made up pay
Benefits	Adult	Incapacity Benefit, receiving made up pay, frequency (every week/only some weeks)
Benefits	Adult	Incapacity benefit, receiving made up pay, number of weeks received
Benefits	Adult	Jobseeker's Allowance, amount received
Benefits	Adult	Jobseeker's Allowance, amount received, period covered
Benefits	Adult	Jobseeker's Allowance, awaiting outcome of a claim
Benefits	Adult	Jobseeker's Allowance, number of weeks received
Benefits	Adult	Jobseeker's Allowance, whether contributions based or income based
Benefits	Adult	Maternity Allowance, amount received
Benefits	Adult	Maternity Allowance, amount received, period covered
Benefits	Adult	Maternity Allowance, how benefit paid (order book, giro etc)
Benefits	Adult	Retirement Pension, amount received
Benefits	Adult	Retirement Pension, amount received, period covered
Benefits	Adult	Retirement Pension, amount usually received
Benefits	Adult	Retirement Pension, amount usually received, period covered
Benefits	Adult	Retirement Pension, how benefit paid (order book, giro etc)
Benefits	Adult	Retirement Pension, whether Attendance Allowance, Disability Allowance (care or mobility components), paid with pension or separately
Benefits	Adult	Retirement Pension, order book codes
Benefits	Adult	Severe Disablement Allowance, amount received
Benefits	Adult	Severe Disablement Allowance, amount received, period covered
Benefits	Adult	Severe Disablement Allowance, how benefit paid (order book, giro etc)
Benefits	Adult	Social Fund Community Care Grant, received in the last 6 months
Benefits	Adult	Social Fund Community Care Grant, received in the last 6 months, amount borrowed altogether
Benefits	Adult	Social Fund Grant for funeral expenses, received in the last 6 months
Benefits	Adult	Social Fund Grant for funeral expenses, received in the last 6 months, amount received
Benefits	Adult	Social Fund Grant for maternity expenses, received in the last 6 months
Benefits	Adult	Social Fund Grant for maternity expenses, received in the last 6 months, amount received
Benefits	Adult	Social Fund Grant for maternity expenses, received in the last 6 months, how benefit paid (order book, giro etc)
Benefits	Adult	Social Fund loans, number of loans in last 6 months
Benefits	Adult	Social Fund loans, amount borrowed altogether
Benefits	Adult	Social Fund loans, whether budgeting or crisis loan
Benefits	Adult	Social Fund repayments, presently being made
Benefits	Adult	Social Fund repayments, presently being made, total repaid per week
Benefits	Adult	Trade union sick or strike pay received in the last 12 months
Benefits	Adult	Trade union sick or strike pay received in the last 12 months, presently receiving
Benefits	Adult	Trade union sick or strike pay received in the last 12 months, presently receiving, amount received
Benefits	Adult	Trade union sick or strike pay received in the last 12 months, presently receiving, amount received, period covered
Benefits	Adult	Trade union sick or strike pay received in the last 12 months, presently receiving, number of weeks in last 12 months received
Benefits	Adult	War Disablement Pension, amount received
Benefits	Adult	War Disablement Pension, amount received, period covered
Benefits	Adult	War Disablement Pension, how benefit paid (order book, giro etc)
Benefits	Adult	War Widow's Pension, amount received
Benefits	Adult	War Widow's Pension, amount received, period covered
Benefits	Adult	War Widow's Pension, how benefit paid (order book, giro etc)
Benefits	Adult	Widowed Mother's Allowance, amount received
Benefits	Adult	Widowed Mother's Allowance, amount received, period covered
Benefits	Adult	Widowed Mother's Allowance, amount usually received
Benefits	Adult	Widowed Mother's Allowance, amount usually received, period covered
Benefits	Adult	Widowed Mother's Allowance, how benefit paid (order book, giro etc)

DSS, Family Resources Survey Great Britain 1999–2000, © Crown Copyright 2001

Benefits	Adult	Widowed Mother's Allowance, order book codes
Benefits	Adult	Widow's Payment (lump sum), amount received
Benefits	Adult	Widow's Pension, amount received
Benefits	Adult	Widow's Pension, amount received, period covered
Benefits	Adult	Widow's Pension, amount usually received
Benefits	Adult	Widow's Pension, amount usually received, period covered
Benefits	Adult	Widow's Pension, how benefit paid (order book, giro etc)
Benefits	Adult	Widow's Pension, order book codes
Pensions and trusts	Adult	Annuity (includes home income plan or equity release), bought with lump sum from employee/personal pension scheme
Pensions and trusts	Adult	Annuity (includes home income plan or equity release), amount of tax deducted at source
Pensions and trusts	Adult	Annuity (includes home income plan or equity release), amount received
Pensions and trusts	Adult	Annuity (includes home income plan or equity release), amount received, period covered
Pensions and trusts	Up to 4 per adult	Employee pension from previous employer, amount of other deductions deducted
Pensions and trusts	Up to 4 per adult	Employee pension from previous employer, amount of tax deducted at source
Pensions and trusts	Up to 4 per adult	Employee pension from previous employer, amount received
Pensions and trusts	Up to 4 per adult	Employee pension from previous employer, amount received, period covered
Pensions and trusts	Up to 3 per adult	Personal pension, amount of tax deducted at source
Pensions and trusts	Up to 3 per adult	Personal pension, amount received
Pensions and trusts	Up to 3 per adult	Personal pension, amount received, period covered
Pensions and trusts	Adult	Redundancy payments received in last 12 months, amount received
Pensions and trusts	Adult	Trade Union or friendly society pension, amount received
Pensions and trusts	Adult	Trade Union or friendly society pension, amount received, period covered
Pensions and trusts	Adult	Trust or covenant, amount of tax deducted at source
Pensions and trusts	Adult	Trust or covenant, amount received
Pensions and trusts	Adult	Trust or covenant, amount received, period covered
Pensions and trusts	Adult	Trust or covenant, rights to income or capital withdrawal (permission required for income/capital only, or both)
Pensions and trusts	Up to 3 per adult	Widow's employee pension, amount of other deductions deducted
Pensions and trusts	Up to 3 per adult	Widow's employee pension, amount of tax deducted at source
Pensions and trusts	Up to 3 per adult	Widow's employee pension, amount received
Pensions and trusts	Up to 3 per adult	Widow's employee pension, amount received, period covered
Royalties and allowances	Adult	Allowances from absent partner, amount received
Royalties and allowances	Adult	Allowances from absent partner, amount received, period covered
	Adult	Allowances from absent partner, direct payments for household expenses, total amount
Royalties and allowances	Adult	Allowances from absent partner, direct payments for household expenses, total amount, period covered
Royalties and allowances	Adult	Income as a sleeping partner in a business, amount received in last 12 months
Royalties and allowances		Occupational pension from an overseas government or company paid in foreign currency, amount received in last 12 months
Royalties and allowances	Adult	Regular allowance from an organisation, amount received
Royalties and allowances	Adult	Regular allowance from an organisation, amount received, period covered
Royalties and allowances	Adult	Regular allowance from a local authority for a foster child, amount received
Royalties and allowances	Adult	Regular allowance from a local authority for a foster child, amount received, period covered
Royalties and allowances	Adult	Regular allowance from a local authority for an adopted child, amount received
Royalties and allowances	Adult	Regular allowance from a local authority for an adopted child, amount received, period covered
Royalties and allowances	Adult	Regular allowance from temporarily absent household member or friend or relative outside the household, amount received
Royalties and allowances	Adult	Regular allowance from temporarily absent household member or friend or relative outside the household, amount received, period covered
Royalties and allowances	Adult	Royalties, amount received in the last 12 months
Maintenance	Up to 4 payments per adult	Maintenance paid, age of youngest child
Maintenance	Up to 4 payments per adult	Maintenance paid, amount of last payment
Maintenance	Up to 4 payments per adult	Maintenance paid, amount of last payment, period covered
Maintenance	Up to 4 payments per adult	Maintenance paid, number of children covered by payment
Maintenance	Up to 4 payments per adult	Maintenance paid, payments covered by court order
Maintenance	Up to 4 payments per adult	Maintenance paid, payments for (former partner only, child(ren), partner and children)
Maintenance	Up to 4 payments per adult	Maintenance paid, usual amount paid (if different)
Maintenance	Up to 4 payments per adult	Maintenance paid, usual amount paid (if different), period covered
Maintenance	Up to 4 payments per adult	Maintenance paid, variation in amount paid since started making payments (up, down, haven't changed)
Maintenance	Up to 4 payments per adult	Maintenance paid, variation in amount paid since started making payments, reason for change
Maintenance	Adult	Maintenance, received, amount in relation to court order/expected (more, less, about the same)
Maintenance	Adult	Maintenance, received, amount of last payment
Maintenance	Adult	Maintenance, received, amount of last payment, period covered
Maintenance	Adult	Maintenance, received, court order requiring previous partner to make money payments (whether actually received or not)
Maintenance	Adult	Maintenance, received, paid to self or via DSS/CSA
Maintenance	Adult	Maintenance, received, payments for (self, child(ren), self and children)

Maintenance	Adult	Maintenance, received, usual amount (if different)
Maintenance	Adult	Maintenance, received, usual amount (if different), period covered
Income tax	Adult	Income tax, payments in last 12 months (apart from those mentioned elsewhere)
Income tax	Adult	Income tax, payments in last 12 months (apart from those mentioned elsewhere), amount paid
NI insurance contribution	Adult	NI insurance, regular contribution (non-employees), amount last paid
NI insurance contribution	Adult	NI insurance, regular contribution (non-employees), amount last paid, period covered
Odd jobs	Up to 3 per adult	Amount received
Odd jobs	Adult	In last 4 weeks, received money for odd jobs or occasional fees for work or professional advice not yet covered
Odd jobs	Adult	Mail order agent or baby-sitting, in last 7 days
Odd jobs	Adult	Mail order agent or baby-sitting, income received in last 4 weeks
Odd jobs	Adult	Mail order agent or baby-sitting, income received in last 4 weeks, amount
Children's earnings	Child	Income from a trust in the last 12 months
Children's earnings	Child	Income from a trust in the last 12 months, amount received last time
Children's earnings	Child	Income from a trust in the last 12 months, amount received last time, period covered
Children's earnings	Child	Income from a trust in the last 12 months, income received throughout the year
Children's earnings	Child	Income from spare time job in the last 12 months
Children's earnings	Child	Income from spare time job in the last 12 months, amount received last time
Children's earnings	Child	Income from spare time job in the last 12 months, amount received last time, period covered
Children's earnings	Child	Income from spare time job in the last 12 months, income received throughout the year
Children's earnings	Child	Income from spare time job in the last 12 months, number of weeks had job in last year
Interest and Dividends	Adult	Any other account/bond with banks/societies, interest received in last 12 months, before/after tax
Interest and Dividends	Adult	Current account with Bank/Building society/other organisation, interest received in last 12 months, before/after tax
Interest and Dividends	Adult	Government Gilt-edged stock (including war loan), interest received in last 12 months, before/after tax
Interest and Dividends	**Adult**	**ISA, interest received in last 12 months**
Interest and Dividends	Adult	NSB/PO Investment Account, interest received in last 12 months, before/after tax
Interest and Dividends	Adult	NSB/PO Ordinary Account, interest received in last 12 months, before/after tax
Interest and Dividends	Adult	PEPs, interest received in the last 12 months
Interest and Dividends	Adult	Stocks, shares, bonds, debentures or other securities, interest received in last 12 months
Interest and Dividends	Adult	TESSA, interest received in last 12 months
Interest and Dividends	Adult	Unit Trusts/Investment Trusts, interest received in last 12 months
Investments	Adult	Fixed Interest National Savings Certificates, money at present held in
Investments	Adult	Index-linked National Savings Certificates, money at present held in
Investments	Adult	National Savings Capital bonds, money at present held in
Investments	Adult	National Savings Deposit Bonds, money at present held in
Investments	Adult	National Savings FIRST Option Bonds, money at present held in
Investments	Adult	National Savings Income Bonds, money at present held in
Investments	Adult	National Savings Yearly Plan, money at present held in
Investments	Adult	Pensioners' Guaranteed Income Bonds, money at present held in
Investments	Adult	Premium Bonds, money at present held in
Investments	Adult	Save-As-You-Earn, money at present held in
Total savings	Benefit unit/Child	Respondent's estimate of total savings in bands
Change in income in last 3 months	Benefit unit	Present income higher/lower/about the same
Change in income in last 3 months	Benefit unit	Present income lower by bands of income per week
National Savings Products	Adults/children not entering the assets block	Banded value of amount of investment (information on value of National Savings Products now collected for all respondents)
Assets	Subset of Adults, up to 4 accounts	Current account with Bank/Building society, amount left at end of last month
Assets	Subset of Adults, up to 10 assets	Government Gilt-edged stock, Unit Trusts, stocks, shares, bonds, amount held in
Assets	**Subset of Adults**	**ISA, amount held in**
Assets	**Subset of Adults**	**ISA, type of (cash, stocks and shares, life insurance)**
Assets	Subset of Adults, up to 5 assets	National Savings Certificates, amount held in
Assets	Subset of Adults, up to 6 assets	National Savings Deposit Bonds, amount held in
Assets	Subset of Adults, up to 6 assets	National Savings Deposit Bonds, date acquired
Assets	Subset of Adults	National Savings FIRST Option Bonds, amount held in
Assets	Subset of Adults	National Savings Income Bonds, amount held in
Assets	Subset of Adults	National Savings Yearly Plan, amount held in
Assets	Subset of Adults	Pensioner Guaranteed Income Bonds, amount held in
Assets	Subset of Adults	Premium Bonds, amount held in
Assets	Subset of Adults, up to 5 assets	Save-As-You-Earn, amount held in
Assets	Subset of Adults, up to 5 assets	Save-As-You-Earn, amount regularly pay

DSS, Family Resources Survey Great Britain 1999-2000, © Crown Copyright 2001

Assets	Subset of Adults, up to 5 assets	Save-As-You-Earn, amount regularly pay, period covered
Assets	Subset of Adults, up to 5 assets	Save-As-You-Earn, date started
Assets	Subset of Adults, up to 5 assets	Save-As-You-Earn, national savings scheme, or bank/building society
Assets	Subset of Adults, up to 7 accounts	Savings account with Bank/Building society, amount held in
Assets	Subset of Adults, up to 7 accounts	Savings account with Bank/Building society, sole or joint account
Assets	Subset of Adults	TESSA, amount held in